Casenote™ Legal Briefs

WILLS, TRUSTS, AND ESTATES

Keyed to Courses Using

**Dukeminier, Johanson, Lindgren, and Sitkoff's
Wills, Trusts, and Estates**

Seventh Edition

PUBLISHERS

111 Eighth Avenue, New York, NY 10011
www.aspenpublishers.com

This publication is designed to provide accurate and authoritative information in regard to the subject matter covered. It is sold with the understanding that the publisher is not engaged in rendering legal, accounting, or other professional services. If legal advice or other expert assistance is required, the services of a competent professional person should be sought.

— From a *Declaration of Principles* adopted jointly by a Committee of the American Bar Association and a Committee of Publishers and Associates

About Aspen Publishers

Aspen Publishers, headquartered in New York City, is a leading information provider for attorneys, business professionals, and law students. Written by preeminent authorities, our products consist of analytical and practical information covering both U.S. and international topics. We publish in the full range of formats, including updated manuals, books, periodicals, CDs, and online products.

Our proprietary content is complemented by 2,500 legal databases, containing over 11 million documents, available through our Loislaw division. Aspen Publishers also offers a wide range of topical legal and business databases linked to Loislaw's primary material. Our mission is to provide accurate, timely, and authoritative content in easily accessible formats, supported by unmatched customer care.

To order any Aspen Publishers title, go to *www.aspenpublishers.com* or call 1-800-638-8437.

For more information on Loislaw products, go to *www.loislaw.com* or call 1-800-364-2512.

For Customer Care issues, e-mail *CustomerCare@aspenpublishers.com*; call 1-800-234-1660; or fax 1-800-901-9075.

Aspen Publishers
a Wolters Kluwer business

Format for the Casenote Legal Brief

Nature of Case: This section identifies the form of action (e.g., breach of contract, negligence, battery), the type of proceeding (e.g., demurrer, appeal from trial court's jury instructions) or the relief sought (e.g., damages, injunction, criminal sanctions).

Fact Summary: This is included to refresh your memory and can be used as a quick reminder of the facts.

Rule of Law: Summarizes the general principle of law that the case illustrates. It may be used for instant recall of the court's holding and for classroom discussion or home review.

Facts: This section contains all relevant facts of the case, including the contentions of the parties and the lower court holdings. It is written in a logical order to give the student a clear understanding of the case. The plaintiff and defendant are identified by their proper names throughout and are always labeled with a (P) or (D).

Party ID: Quick identification of the relationship between the parties.

Concurrence/Dissent: All concurrences and dissents are briefed whenever they are included by the casebook editor.

Analysis: This last paragraph gives you a broad understanding of where the case "fits in" with other cases in the section of the book and with the entire course. It is a hornbook-style discussion indicating whether the case is a majority or minority opinion and comparing the principal case with other cases in the casebook. It may also provide analysis from restatements, uniform codes, and law review articles. The analysis will prove to be invaluable to classroom discussion.

Palsgraf v. Long Island R.R. Co.

Injured bystander (P) v. Railroad company (D)

N.Y. Ct. App., 248 N.Y. 339, 162 N.E. 99 (1928).

NATURE OF CASE: Appeal from judgment affirming verdict for plaintiff seeking damages for personal injury.

FACT SUMMARY: Helen Palsgraf (P) was injured on R.R.'s (D) train platform when R.R.'s (D) guard helped a passenger aboard a moving train, causing his package to fall on the tracks. The package contained fireworks which exploded, creating a shock that tipped a scale onto Palsgraf (P).

🏛 RULE OF LAW
The risk reasonably to be perceived defines the duty to be obeyed.

FACTS: Helen Palsgraf (P) purchased a ticket to Rockaway Beach from R.R. (D) and was waiting on the train platform. As she waited, two men ran to catch a train that was pulling out from the platform. The first man jumped aboard, but the second man, who appeared as if he might fall, was helped aboard by the guard on the train who had kept the door open so they could jump aboard. A guard on the platform also helped by pushing him onto the train. The man was carrying a package wrapped in newspaper. In the process, the man dropped his package, which fell on the tracks. The package contained fireworks and exploded. The shock of the explosion was apparently of great enough strength to tip over some scales at the other end of the platform, which fell on Palsgraf (P) and injured her. A jury awarded her damages, and R.R. (D) appealed.

ISSUE: Does the risk reasonably to be perceived define the duty to be obeyed?

HOLDING AND DECISION: (Cardozo, C.J.) Yes. The risk reasonably to be perceived defines the duty to be obeyed. If there is no foreseeable hazard to the injured party as the result of a seemingly innocent act, the act does not become a tort because it happened to be a wrong as to another. If the wrong was not willful, the plaintiff must show that the act as to her had such great and apparent possibilities of danger as to entitle her to protection. Negligence in the abstract is not enough upon which to base liability. Negligence is a relative concept, evolving out of the common law doctrine of trespass on the case. To establish liability, the defendant must owe a legal duty of reasonable care to the injured party. A cause of action in tort will lie where harm, though unintended, could

have been averted or avoided by observance of such a duty. The scope of the duty is limited by the range of danger that a reasonable person could foresee. In this case, there was nothing to suggest from the appearance of the parcel or otherwise that the parcel contained fireworks. The guard could not reasonably have had any warning of a threat to Palsgraf (P), and R.R. (D) therefore cannot be held liable. Judgment is reversed in favor of R.R. (D).

DISSENT: (Andrews, J.) The concept that there is no negligence unless R.R. (D) owes a legal duty to take care as to Palsgraf (P) herself is too narrow. Everyone owes to the world at large the duty of refraining from those acts that may unreasonably threaten the safety of others. If the guard's action was negligent as to those nearby, it was also negligent as to those outside what might be termed the "danger zone." For Palsgraf (P) to recover, R.R.'s (D) negligence must have been the proximate cause of her injury, a question of fact for the jury.

▶ ANALYSIS

The majority defined the limit of the defendant's liability in terms of the danger that a reasonable person in defendant's situation would have perceived. The dissent argued that the limitation should not be placed on liability, but rather on damages. Judge Andrews suggested that only injuries that would not have happened but for R.R.'s (D) negligence should be compensable. Both the majority and dissent recognized the policy-driven need to limit liability for negligent acts, seeking, in the words of Judge Andrews, to define a framework "that will be practical and in keeping with the general understanding of mankind." The Restatement (Second) of Torts has accepted Judge Cardozo's view.

Quicknotes

FORESEEABILITY A reasonable expectation that change is the probable result of certain acts or omissions.

NEGLIGENCE Conduct falling below the standard of care that a reasonable person would demonstrate under similar conditions.

PROXIMATE CAUSE The natural sequence of events without which an injury would not have been sustained.

Issue: The issue is a concise question that brings out the essence of the opinion as it relates to the section of the casebook in which the case appears. Both substantive and procedural issues are included if relevant to the decision.

Holding and Decision: This section offers a clear and in-depth discussion of the rule of the case and the court's rationale. It is written in easy-to-understand language and answers the issues(s) presented by applying the law to the facts of the case. When relevant, it includes a thorough discussion of the exceptions to the case as listed by the court, any major cites to the other cases on point, and the names of the judges who wrote the decisions.

Quicknotes: Conveniently defines legal terms found in the case and summarizes the nature of any statutes, codes, or rules referred to in the text.

Note to Students

Aspen Publishers is proud to offer *Casenote Legal Briefs*—continuing thirty years of publishing America's best-selling legal briefs.

Casenote Legal Briefs are designed to help you save time when briefing assigned cases. Organized under convenient headings, they show you how to abstract the basic facts and holdings from the text of the actual opinions handed down by the courts. Used as part of a rigorous study regime, they can help you spend more time analyzing and critiquing points of law than on copying out bits and pieces of judicial opinions into your notebook or outline.

Casenote Legal Briefs should never be used as a substitute for assigned casebook readings. They work best when read as a follow-up to reviewing the underlying opinions themselves. Students who try to avoid reading and digesting the judicial opinions in their casebooks or on-line sources will end up shortchanging themselves in the long run. The ability to absorb, critique, and restate the dynamic and complex elements of case law decisions is crucial to your success in law school and beyond. It cannot be developed vicariously.

Casenote Legal Briefs represent but one of the many offerings in Aspen's Study Aid Timeline, which includes:

- Casenote *Legal Briefs*
- Emanuel *Law Outlines*
- *Examples & Explanations* Series
- *Introduction to Law* Series
- Emanuel *Law in a Flash* Flashcards
- Emanuel *CrunchTime* Series

Each of these series is designed to provide you with easy-to-understand explanations of complex points of law. Each volume offers guidance on the principles of legal analysis and, consulted regularly, will hone your ability to spot relevant issues. We have titles that will help you prepare for class, prepare for your exams, and enhance your general comprehension of the law along the way.

To find out more about Aspen Study Aid publications, visit us on-line at *www.aspenpublishers.com* or e-mail us at *legaledu@aspenpubl.com*. We'll be happy to assist you.

Free access to Briefs on-line!

Download the cases you want in your notes or outlines using the full cut-and-paste feature accompanying our on-line briefs. Please fill out this form for full access to this useful feature. No photocopies of this form will be accepted.

Name	Phone ( )

Address	Apt. No.

City	State	ZIP Code

Law School	Year (check one) ☐ 1st ☐ 2nd ☐ 3rd

Cut out the UPC found on the lower left-hand corner of the back cover of this book. Staple the UPC inside this box. Only the original UPC from the book cover will be accepted. No photocopies or store stickers are allowed.

Attach UPC inside this box.

E-mail (Print LEGIBLY or you may not get access!)

Title of this book (course subject)

Used with which casebook (provide author's name)

Mail the completed form to: Aspen Publishers, Inc.
Legal Education Division
Casenote On-line Access
130 Turner Street, Building 3 - 4th Floor
Waltham, MA 02453

I understand that on-line access is granted solely to the purchaser of this book for the academic year in which it was purchased. Any other usage is not authorized and will result in immediate termination of access. Sharing of codes is strictly prohibited.

Signature _____

Upon receipt of this completed form, you will be e-mailed codes so that you may access the Briefs for this Casenote Legal Brief. On-line Briefs may not be available for all titles. For a full list of available titles, please check *www.aspenpublishers.com/casenotes.*

A. Decide on a Format and Stick to It

Structure is essential to a good brief. It enables you to arrange systematically the related parts that are scattered throughout most cases, thus making manageable and understandable what might otherwise seem to be an endless and unfathomable sea of information. There are, of course, an unlimited number of formats that can be utilized. However, it is best to find one that suits your needs and stick to it. Consistency breeds both efficiency and the security that when called upon you will know where to look in your brief for the information you are asked to give.

Any format, as long as it presents the essential elements of a case in an organized fashion, can be used. Experience, however, has led *Casenotes* to develop and utilize the following format because of its logical flow and universal applicability.

NATURE OF CASE: This is a brief statement of the legal character and procedural status of the case (e.g., "Appeal of a burglary conviction").

There are many different alternatives open to a litigant dissatisfied with a court ruling. The key to determining which one has been used is to discover *who is asking this court for what.*

This first entry in the brief should be kept *as short as possible.* Use the court's terminology if you understand it. But since jurisdictions vary as to the titles of pleadings, the best entry is the one that addresses who wants what in this proceeding, not the one that sounds most like the court's language.

RULE OF LAW: A statement of the general principle of law that the case illustrates (e.g., "An acceptance that varies any term of the offer is considered a rejection and counter-offer").

Determining the rule of law of a case is a procedure similar to determining the issue of the case. Avoid being fooled by red herrings; there may be a few rules of law mentioned in the case excerpt, but usually only one is *the* rule with which the casebook editor is concerned. The techniques used to locate the issue, described below, may also be utilized to find the rule of law. Generally, your best guide is simply the chapter heading. It is a clue to the point the casebook editor seeks to make and should be kept in mind when reading every case in the respective section.

FACTS: A synopsis of only the essential facts of the case, i.e., those bearing upon or leading up to the issue.

The facts entry should be a short statement of the events and transactions that led one party to initiate legal proceedings against another in the first place. While some cases conveniently state the salient facts at the beginning of the decision, in other instances they will have to be culled from hiding places throughout the text, even from concurring and dissenting opinions. Some of the "facts" will often be in dispute and should be so noted. Conflicting evidence may be briefly pointed up. "Hard" facts must be included. Both must be *relevant* in order to be listed in the facts entry. It is impossible to tell what is relevant until the entire case is read, as the ultimate determination of the rights and liabilities of the parties may turn on something buried deep in the opinion.

Generally, the facts entry should not be longer than three to five *short* sentences.

It is often helpful to identify the role played by a party in a given context. For example, in a construction contract case the identification of a party as the "contractor" or "builder" alleviates the need to tell that that party was the one who was supposed to have built the house.

It is always helpful, and a good general practice, to identify the "plaintiff" and the "defendant." This may seem elementary and uncomplicated, but, especially in view of the creative editing practiced by some casebook editors, it is sometimes a difficult or even impossible task. Bear in mind that the *party presently* seeking something from this court may not be the plaintiff, and that sometimes only the cross-claim of a defendant is treated in the excerpt. Confusing or misaligning the parties can ruin your analysis and understanding of the case.

ISSUE: A statement of the general legal question answered by or illustrated in the case. For clarity, the issue is best put in the form of a question capable of a "yes" or "no" answer. In reality, the issue is simply the Rule of Law put in the form of a question (e.g., "May an offer be accepted by performance?").

The major problem presented in discerning what is *the* issue in the case is that an opinion usually purports to raise and answer several questions. However, except for rare cases, only one such question is really the issue in the case. Collateral issues not necessary to the resolution of the matter in controversy are handled by the court by language known as *"obiter dictum"* or merely *"dictum."* While dicta may be included later in the brief, they have no place under the issue heading.

To find the issue, ask *who wants what* and then go on to ask *why did that party succeed or fail in getting it.* Once this is determined, the "why" should be turned into a question.

The complexity of the issues in the cases will vary, but in all cases a single-sentence question should sum up the issue.

In a few cases, there will be two, or even more rarely, three issues of equal importance to the resolution of the case. Each should be expressed in a single-sentence question.

Since many issues are resolved by a court in coming to a final disposition of a case, the casebook editor will reproduce the portion of the opinion containing the issue or issues most relevant to the area of law under scrutiny. A noted law professor gave this advice: "Close the book; look at the title on the cover." Chances are, if it is Property, you need not concern yourself with whether, for example, the federal government's treatment of the plaintiff's land really raises a federal question sufficient to support jurisdiction on this ground in federal court.

The same rule applies to chapter headings designating sub-areas within the subjects. They tip you off as to what the text is designed to teach. The cases are arranged in a casebook to show a progression or development of the law, so that the preceding cases may also help.

It is also most important to remember to *read the notes and questions* at the end of a case to determine what the editors wanted you to have gleaned from it.

HOLDING AND DECISION: This section should succinctly explain the rationale of the court in arriving at its decision. In capsulizing the "reasoning" of the court, it should always include an application of the general rule or rules of law to the specific facts of the case. Hidden justifications come to light in this entry; the reasons for the state of the law, the public policies, the biases and prejudices, those considerations that influence the justices' thinking and, ultimately, the outcome of the case. At the end, there should be a short indication of the disposition or procedural resolution of the case (e.g., "Decision of the trial court for Mr. Smith (P) reversed").

The foregoing format is designed to help you "digest" the reams of case material with which you will be faced in your law school career. Once mastered by practice, it will place at your fingertips the information the authors of your casebooks have sought to impart to you in case-by-case illustration and analysis.

B. Be as Economical as Possible in Briefing Cases

Once armed with a format that encourages succinctness, it is as important to be economical with regard to the time spent on the actual reading of the case as it is to be economical in the writing of the brief itself. This does not mean "skimming" a case. Rather, it means reading the case with an "eye" trained to recognize into which "section" of your brief a particular passage or line fits and having a system for quickly and precisely marking the case so that the passages fitting any one particular part of the brief can be easily identified and brought together in a concise and accurate manner when the brief is actually written.

It is of no use to simply repeat everything in the opinion of the court; record only enough information to trigger your recollection of what the court said. Nevertheless, an accurate statement of the "law of the case," i.e., the legal principle applied to the facts, is absolutely essential to class preparation and to learning the law under the case method.

To that end, it is important to develop a "shorthand" that you can use to make margin notations. These notations will tell you at a glance in which section of the brief you will be placing that particular passage or portion of the opinion.

Some students prefer to underline all the salient portions of the opinion (with a pencil or colored underliner marker), making marginal notations as they go along. Others prefer the color-coded method of underlining, utilizing different colors of markers to underline the salient portions of the case, each separate color being used to represent a different section of the brief. For example, blue underlining could be used for passages relating to the rule of law, yellow for those relating to the issue, and green for those relating to the holding and decision, etc. While it has its advocates, the color-coded method can be confusing and time-consuming (all that time spent on changing colored markers). Furthermore, it can interfere with the continuity and concentration many students deem essential to the reading of a case for maximum comprehension. In the end, however, it is a matter of personal preference and style. Just remember, whatever method you use, underlining must be used sparingly or its value is lost.

If you take the marginal notation route, an efficient and easy method is to go along underlining the key portions of the case and placing in the margin alongside them the following "markers" to indicate where a particular passage or line "belongs" in the brief you will write:

N   (NATURE OF CASE)
RL   (RULE OF LAW)
I   (ISSUE)
HL   (HOLDING AND DECISION, relates to the RULE OF LAW behind the decision)
HR   (HOLDING AND DECISION, gives the RATIONALE or reasoning behind the decision)
HA   (HOLDING AND DECISION, APPLIES the general principle(s) of law to the facts of the case to arrive at the decision)

Remember that a particular passage may well contain information necessary to more than one part of your brief, in which case you simply note that in the margin. If you are using the color-coded underlining method instead of margin notation, simply make asterisks or checks in the margin next to the passage in question in the colors that indicate the additional sections of the brief where it might be utilized.

The economy of utilizing "shorthand" in marking cases for briefing can be maintained in the actual brief writing process itself by utilizing "law student shorthand" within the brief. There are many commonly used words and phrases for which abbreviations can be substituted in your briefs (and in your class notes also). You can develop abbreviations that are personal to you and which will save you a lot of time. A reference list of briefing abbreviations can be found on page xii of this book.

C. Use Both the Briefing Process and the Brief as a Learning Tool

Now that you have a format and the tools for briefing cases efficiently, the most important thing is to make the time spent in briefing profitable to you and to make the most advantageous use of the briefs you create. Of course, the briefs are invaluable for classroom reference when you are called upon to explain or analyze a particular case. However, they are also useful in reviewing for exams. A quick glance at the fact summary should bring the case to mind, and a rereading of the rule of law should enable you to go over the underlying legal concept in your mind, how it was applied in that particular case, and how it might apply in other factual settings.

As to the value to be derived from engaging in the briefing process itself, there is an immediate benefit that arises from being forced to sift through the essential facts and reasoning from the court's opinion and to succinctly express them in your own words in your brief. The process ensures that you understand the case and the point that it illustrates, and that means you will be ready to absorb further analysis and information brought forth in class. It also ensures you will have something to say when called upon in class. The briefing process helps develop a mental agility for getting to the *gist* of a case and for identifying, expounding on, and applying the legal concepts and issues found there. The briefing process is the mental process on which you must rely in taking law school examinations; it is also the mental process upon which a lawyer relies in serving his clients and in making his living.

Abbreviations for Briefs

acceptance	acp	offer	O
affirmed	aff	offeree	OE
answer	ans	offeror	OR
assumption of risk	a/r	ordinance	ord
attorney	atty	pain and suffering	p/s
beyond a reasonable doubt	b/r/d	parol evidence	p/e
bona fide purchaser	BFP	plaintiff	P
breach of contract	br/k	prima facie	p/f
cause of action	c/a	probable cause	p/c
common law	c/l	proximate cause	px/c
Constitution	Con	real property	r/p
constitutional	con	reasonable doubt	r/d
contract	K	reasonable man	r/m
contributory negligence	c/n	rebuttable presumption	rb/p
cross	x	remanded	rem
cross-complaint	x/c	res ipsa loquitur	RIL
cross-examination	x/ex	respondeat superior	r/s
cruel and unusual punishment	c/u/p	Restatement	RS
defendant	D	reversed	rev
dismissed	dis	Rule Against Perpetuities	RAP
double jeopardy	d/j	search and seizure	s/s
due process	d/p	search warrant	s/w
equal protection	e/p	self-defense	s/d
equity	eq	specific performance	s/p
evidence	ev	statute of limitations	S/L
exclude	exc	statute of frauds	S/F
exclusionary rule	exc/r	statute	S
felony	f/n	summary judgment	s/j
freedom of speech	f/s	tenancy in common	t/c
good faith	g/f	tenancy at will	t/w
habeas corpus	h/c	tenant	t
hearsay	hr	third party	TP
husband	H	third party beneficiary	TPB
in loco parentis	ILP	transferred intent	TI
injunction	inj	unconscionable	uncon
inter vivos	I/v	unconstitutional	unconst
joint tenancy	j/t	undue influence	u/e
judgment	judgt	Uniform Commercial Code	UCC
jurisdiction	jur	unilateral	uni
last clear chance	LCC	vendee	VE
long-arm statute	LAS	vendor	VR
majority view	maj	versus	v
meeting of minds	MOM	void for vagueness	VFV
minority view	min	weight of the evidence	w/e
Miranda warnings	Mir/w	weight of authority	w/a
Miranda rule	Mir/r	wife	W
negligence	neg	with	w/
notice	ntc	within	w/i
nuisance	nus	without prejudice	w/o/p
obligation	ob	without	w/o
obscene	obs	wrongful death	wr/d

Table of Cases

Introduction to Estate Planning

Quick Reference Rules of Law

Hodel v. Irving

Secretary of the Interior (D) v. Sioux Indian (P)

481 U.S. 704 (1987).

NATURE OF CASE: Appeal from judgment finding a statute unconstitutional as a taking without just compensation.

FACT SUMMARY: Congress enacted the Indian Land Consolidation Act, which contained a provision that certain fractional interests owned by tribe members would escheat to the tribe.

RULE OF LAW
The complete abolition of the rights of an owner to dispose of property rights is a taking without just compensation, violating the owner's rights guaranteed under the Fifth Amendment.

FACTS: The Indian Land Acts enacted at the end of the nineteenth century provided that each Sioux Indian was allotted reservation land which was held in trust by the United States. Eventually the lands were splintered into multiple undivided interests, with some parcels having hundreds of fractional owners. In 1983, Congress passed the Indian Land Consolidation Act. Section 207 of the Act provided that certain fractional interests could not be transferred by intestacy or devise but would escheat to the tribe. No provision was made for the payment of compensation to the owners of the escheated fractional interests. Irving (P), a member of the Sioux tribe and a prospective recipient of one of the fractional interests affected by the statute, filed suit, claiming that § 207 was a taking without just compensation in violation of the Fifth Amendment. The district court found that the statute was constitutional. The court of appeals reversed and declared the statute unconstitutional. Hodel (D), the Secretary of the Interior, appealed.

ISSUE: Is the complete abolition of the rights of an owner to dispose of property rights a taking without just compensation, violating rights guaranteed under the Fifth Amendment?

HOLDING AND DECISION: (O'Connor, J.) Yes. Section 207 amounts to a virtual abrogation of the right to pass a certain type of property—the small undivided interest to one's heirs. A right to pass property to one's family has been part of the Anglo-Saxon legal system since feudal times. The escheatable interests are not necessarily de minimis. Even though the fractional owners have the right to make inter vivos transfers of the interests, such a retained right does not

obviate the total abrogation of the owner's rights to devise the property. Affirmed.

⦿ ANALYSIS

In an analogous case, the Supreme Court upheld the constitutionality of a provision of the Bald Eagle Protection Act, which prohibits the right to sell or trade artifacts made from eagle feathers and eagle parts. *Andrus v. Allard*, 444 U.S. 31 (1979). The Court held that "where an owner possesses a full 'bundle' of property rights, the destruction of one 'strand' of the bundle is not a taking, because the aggregate must be viewed in its entirety." The Court pointed out that the artifact owners could still donate or devise the artifacts.

■■■

Quicknotes

INTER VIVOS TRANSFER A transfer of property that is effectuated between living persons.

JUST COMPENSATION The right guaranteed by the Fifth Amendment to the United States Constitution of a person, when his property is taken for public use by the state, to receive adequate compensation in order to restore him to the position he enjoyed prior to the appropriation.

TAKING A governmental action that substantially deprives an owner of the use and enjoyment of his or her property, requiring compensation.

■■■

Shapira v. Union National Bank

Beneficiary (P) v. Bank (D)

Common Pleas Ct. of Mahoning County, 39 Ohio Misc. 28, 315 N.E.2d 825 (1974).

NATURE OF CASE: Declaratory judgment action.

FACT SUMMARY: Daniel's (P) interest under his father's will was conditioned on the requirement that he marry a Jew whose parents were both Jewish within seven years of his father's death.

RULE OF LAW
A testator may validly impose a restraint on the religion of the spouse of a beneficiary as a condition precedent to inheriting under the will.

FACTS: Under Shapira's will, his son Daniel (P) could only inherit if he was married to a Jewish woman whose parents were both Jewish at the date of Shapira's death or within seven years thereafter. Daniel (P) sought a declaration that the will was unconstitutional since it restricted his right to marry or that such a clause violated public policy.

ISSUE: May a testator attempt to restrict the right of a beneficiary to marry within a certain religion?

HOLDING AND DECISION: (Henderson, J.) Yes. The right to receive property by will is a matter of statutory law. A testator may either disinherit his children or condition their taking in any manner without offending the Constitution. While the right to marry is a constitutionally protected right, there is no state action present herein which would trigger the Due Process or Equal Protection Clause. The courts are not being asked to enforce covenants. The only official action involves the probate of the will, and this is, in itself, insufficient to be deemed state action. Therefore, a testator may restrict a beneficiary's right to marriage without offending the Constitution. Public policy does not prohibit a limited restriction on the right to marriage restricted to members of one religion. A partial restraint of marriage which imposes only reasonable restrictions is not void as violative of public policy. Gifts conditioned on marrying within a certain religious grouping are deemed reasonable restrictions in a majority of jurisdictions. We find that it is not violative of public policy to condition a bequest on the marriage to one of a particular religion. The clause is valid, and Daniel (P) is bound by its terms.

ANALYSIS

A condition requiring the beneficiary not to marry a member of a specific religion is also deemed valid. *In re Clayton's*

Estate, 13 Pa. 413. Where the restriction based on religion unreasonably limits the beneficiary's right to marriage, it will be deemed void, e.g., *Maddox v. Maddox*, 52 Va. 11 (1854), where there were only 4 or 5 unmarried members of the particular sect.

Quicknotes

BENEFICIARY A third party who is the recipient of the benefit of a transaction undertaken by another.

DUE PROCESS The constitutional mandate requiring the courts to protect and enforce individuals' rights and liberties consistent with prevailing principals of fairness and justice and prohibiting the federal and state governments from such activities that deprive its citizens of a life, liberty or property interest.

EQUAL PROTECTION A constitutional guarantee that no person shall be denied the same protection of the laws enjoyed by other persons in life circumstances.

TESTATOR One who executes a will.

Simpson v. Calivas

Will beneficiary (P) v. Attorney (D)

N.H. Sup. Ct., 139 N.H. 1, 650 A.2d 318 (1994).

NATURE OF CASE: Appeal from summary judgment and dismissal of negligence and breach of contract action.

FACT SUMMARY: Calivas (D) drafted a will for Robert Simpson Sr. that was intended to leave property to his son, but was ambiguous, causing Robert Jr. (P) to bring suit.

🏛 RULE OF LAW
Attorneys drafting wills owe a duty of reasonable care to the intended beneficiaries.

FACTS: In March 1984, Robert Simpson Sr. executed a will that had been drafted by Calivas (D). The will was ambiguously written causing the probate court to award a life estate in Simpson's property to Robert Simpson Jr.'s (P) stepmother, although notes from meetings with Calivas (D) showed that the intent was for Simpson Jr. (P) to receive the entire interest. Since Simpson Jr. (P) had to pay his stepmother $400,000 for the life estate, he sued Calivas (D) for malpractice in improperly drafting the will of his father. The trial court dismissed the action and Simpson Jr. (P) appealed.

ISSUE: Do attorneys drafting wills owe a duty of reasonable care to the intended beneficiaries?

HOLDING AND DECISION: (Horton, J.) Yes. Attorneys drafting wills owe a duty of reasonable care to the intended beneficiaries. In order to recover for negligence a plaintiff must show that the defendant owed a duty of care. Generally, duty arises out of relation between the parties and the scope of such a duty is limited to those in privity of contract. However, there are exceptions to this privity rule. One such exception has been accepted by the overwhelming majority of jurisdictions: attorneys owe a duty to the intended beneficiary of a will. This exception to privity is accepted because of the obvious forseeability of injury upon malpractice. Accordingly, in the present case, the trial court should not have dismissed Simpson Jr.'s (P) negligence action. Reversed.

▶ ANALYSIS

The court also rejected Calivas's (D) argument that collateral estoppel barred the suit. The court found that the probate court had not expressly ruled on the question of Simpson Sr.'s (P) actual intent. Another situation in which privity is not required is where investigators for insurance companies look into claims of the insureds.

■==■

Quicknotes

COLLATERAL ESTOPPEL A doctrine whereby issues litigated and determined in a prior proceeding are binding upon all subsequent litigation between the parties regarding that issue.

DUTY OF REASONABLE CARE Duty to exercise the degree of care as would a reasonably prudent person under like circumstances.

■==■

Hotz v. Minyard

Sister (P) v. Brother (D)

S.C. Sup. Ct., 304 S.C. 225, 403 S.E.2d 634 (1991).

NATURE OF CASE: Appeal from summary judgment in action for breach of fiduciary duty.

FACT SUMMARY: Dobson (D) worked as an attorney for the Minyard family and prepared two wills for Mr. Minyard. He did not tell daughter Judy (P) about the existence of the second will while counseling her on related matters.

> ## RULE OF LAW
> Attorneys may owe a fiduciary duty to the beneficiaries of wills they have prepared.

FACTS: Mr. Minyard owned two car dealerships, at which his children Tommy (D) and Judy (P) worked. Dobson (D), an attorney and accountant, worked for the Minyard family and their business. In 1984, he drafted two wills for Mr. Minyard, who asked Dobson (D) not to reveal the terms of the second will, which was nearly the same as the first except that it gave real estate outright to Tommy (D). Dobson (D) discussed the terms of the first will with Judy (P) and told her that she would be receiving an equal share of the dealerships with her brother even though the first will was actually revoked. After a falling out with her brother over the operation of the business, Judy (P) filed suit against him and Dobson (D) for misleading her about her status under the will. The trial judge granted summary judgment to Dobson (D) on the issue of his duty to Judy (P), and she appealed.

ISSUE: May attorneys owe a fiduciary duty to the beneficiaries of wills they have prepared?

HOLDING AND DECISION: (Gregory, J.) Yes. Attorneys may owe a fiduciary duty to the beneficiaries of wills they have prepared. A fiduciary relationship exists when one party has a special confidence in another so that the other is bound to act in good faith. Although Dobson (D) represented Mr. Minyard, and not Judy (P), with regard to the will, he did have an ongoing legal relationship with Judy (P). Thus, while he had no duty to disclose the second will, Dobson (D) owed a duty to deal with her in good faith and not actively misrepresent the situation. Accordingly, summary judgment was inappropriate on this issue. Reversed and remanded.

▶ ANALYSIS

The court also held that there was a jury question over whether Dobson's (D) law firm could be held vicariously liable. The court did rule that Dobson's (D) accounting firm was off the hook because he was not acting as an accountant during any of the relevant meetings. This case points up the potential morass of representing both the testator and the intended beneficiaries of a will.

Quicknotes

FIDUCIARY DUTY A legal obligation to act for the benefit of another, including subordinating one's personal interests to that of the other person.

TESTATOR One who executes a will.

CHAPTER **2**

Intestacy: An Estate Plan by Default

Quick Reference Rules of Law

Janus v. Tarasewicz

Contingent beneficiary (P) v. Primary beneficiary (D)

Ill. App. Ct., 1st Dist., 135 Ill. App. 3d 936, 482 N.E.2d 418 (1985).

NATURE OF CASE: Appeal from declaratory judgment.

FACT SUMMARY: Stanley and Theresa Janus died after ingesting cyanide-laced Tylenol capsules.

🏛 RULE OF LAW
The determination of legal death must be made in accordance with the usual and customary standards of medical practice.

FACTS: Stanley and Theresa Janus, a married couple, unknowingly took Tylenol capsules laced with cyanide. Soon afterward, Stanley collapsed. Within minutes, Theresa started experiencing seizures. They were both taken to the hospital. Stanley had no blood pressure, pulse, or signs of respiration. Therefore, the medical director at the hospital pronounced him dead on September 29, 1982. Like Stanley, Theresa at first exhibited no visible vital signs when she was admitted to the hospital. However, hospital personnel were able to get her heart beating on its own again and could detect a measurable, though unsatisfactory, blood pressure. Theresa was judged to be in a deep coma with very unstable vital signs and placed in the intensive care ward. One entry in her records indicated that a nurse detected a minimal reaction to light in Theresa's right pupil. On September 30, 1982, various tests were conducted to determine her brain function. As a result of these tests, Theresa was diagnosed as having sustained total brain death and was pronounced dead on October 1, 1982. The proceeds of a life insurance policy on Stanley's life was paid to the administrator of Theresa's estate. Eventually, Theresa's father, Jan Tarasewicz (D) received the life insurance proceeds as Theresa's heir. Alojza Janus (P), Stanley's mother and the contingent beneficiary on Stanley's life insurance policy, sued Tarasewicz (D) for the proceeds. The court concluded from the evidence that Theresa survived Stanley. Janus (P) appealed, contending that there was not sufficient evidence to prove that both victims did not suffer brain death prior to their arrival to the hospital.

ISSUE: Must the determination of legal death be made in accordance with the usual and customary standards of medical practice?

HOLDING AND DECISION: (O'Connor, J.) Yes. The determination of legal death must be made in accordance with the usual and customary standards of medical practice. Both victims arrived at the hospital with artificial respirators and no obvious vital signs. There is no dispute that Stanley Janus died in both a cardiopulmonary sense and a brain death sense when his vital signs disappeared on route to the hospital and were never reestablished. In contrast, hospital personnel were able to reestablish a spontaneous blood pressure and pulse in Theresa. Efforts to preserve Theresa's life continued after more intensive efforts on Stanley's behalf had failed. In the medical director's opinion, Theresa's condition did not warrant a diagnosis of brain death, and she did not suffer irreversible brain death until much later. The record clearly establishes that the treating physician's diagnoses of death with respect to Stanley and Theresa Janus were made within the usual and customary standards of medical practice. Affirmed.

▶ ANALYSIS

The Uniform Probate Code provides that an heir or devisee who fails to survive by 120 hours is deemed to have predeceased the decedent. Attorneys provide for the "no sufficient evidence" problem by providing in a will the following language: "if any person dies with me in a common disaster, any property given to such person by this will shall pass as if such person predeceased me."

■=■

Quicknotes

CONTINGENT BENEFICIARY A third party who is the recipient of the benefit of a transaction undertaken by another, the receipt of which is based on the uncertain happening of another event.

PRIMARY BENEFICIARY The individual specified in a life insurance policy to receive the proceeds upon the insured's death.

SURVIVORSHIP Between two or more persons, such as in a joint tenancy relationship, the right to the property of a deceased passes to the survivor.

■=■

Hall v. Vallandingham

Parties not identified.

Md. Ct. Spec. App., 75 Md. App. 187, 540 A.2d 1162 (1988).

NATURE OF CASE: Appeal from judgment disinheriting relatives.

FACT SUMMARY: After Earl Vallandingham died, his children were adopted by Killgore, his wife's new husband.

RULE OF LAW
An adopted child is no longer considered a child of either natural parent and loses on adoption all rights of inheritance from his natural parents.

FACTS: Earl Vallandingham died, survived by his wife Elizabeth and their four children, Elizabeth married Jim Killgore. Killgore adopted Vallandingham's children. Earl's brother William died childless, unmarried, and intestate. His sole heirs were his surviving brothers and the children of brothers (like Earl) and sisters who predeceased him. Earl's children alleged that they were entitled to their distributive share. The court held that they were not entitled to inherit from William because they had been adopted by Killgore. They appealed.

ISSUE: Is an adopted child no longer considered a child of either natural parent, and does he lose on adoption all rights of inheritance from his natural parents?

HOLDING AND DECISION: (Gilbert, C.J.) Yes. An adopted child is no longer considered a child of either natural parent and loses on adoption all rights of inheritance from his natural parents. The Maryland Estates and Trust Code provides that on adoption, "a child no longer shall be considered a child of either natural parent." To construe this statute so as to allow dual inheritance would bestow upon an adopted child a superior status. Because an adopted child has no right to inherit from the estate of a natural parent who dies intestate, it follows that the same child may not inherit through the natural parent by way of representation. Affirmed.

ANALYSIS

The states disagree whether or not a child continues to have inheritance rights from both natural parents when the child is adopted by a step-parent. Only a few states draw a distinction between adoption of a minor and adoption of an adult. Adult adoption has been used increasingly more frequently to prevent will contests.

Quicknotes

MARYLAND ESTATES AND TRUSTS CODE ANN. § 1-207(A) An adopted child shall be treated as a natural child of his adopted parent or parents. On adoption, a child no longer shall be considered a child of either natural parent, except that upon adoption by the spouse of a natural parent. The child shall be considered the child of that natural parent.

Minary v. Citizens Fidelity Bank & Trust Co.

Daughter-in-law of deceased (P) v. Trustee (D)

Ky. Ct. App., 419 S.W.2d 340 (1967).

NATURE OF CASE: Action seeking to have a will provision construed.

FACT SUMMARY: Amelia Minary placed property in trust for eventual distribution "to [her] then-surviving heirs." One of Amelia's sons adopted his own wife (P), but the Bank (D) refused to distribute the trust property to the wife (P) as Amelia's heir.

🏛 RULE OF LAW
One who adopts a spouse or other adult cannot thereby make the adoptee an heir to an estate created by an existing testamentary instrument executed by an ancestor of the adopter.

FACTS: Amelia Minary's will created a trust, the income of which was to be paid to her husband and her three sons. Upon the death of the last surviving beneficiary, the property which Amelia had placed in the trust was to be distributed "to [her] then-surviving heirs, according to the laws of descent and distribution then in force in Kentucky, and, if no such heirs, then to the First Christian Church, Louisville, Kentucky." Amelia died in 1932. Her husband passed away three years later. Two of her three sons had predeceased their father and had left no issue. Amelia's husband was survived by the couple's daughter and by Alfred, the last of the three sons who had been named beneficiaries of Amelia's trust. In 1934, Alfred married and, prior to his death, adopted his wife (P). When Alfred died in 1959, Myra (P), the wife, demanded that the Citizens Fidelity Bank & Trust Co. (D), the trustee, distribute the corpus of Amelia's trust to her. A suit was eventually filed in which Myra (P) claimed to be, by virtue of having been adopted as Alfred's child, an heir of Amelia Minary. The trial court ruled that Myra (P) was an heir of Amelia, but the trustee (D) appealed.

ISSUE: May a party, by adopting her, make his spouse an heir of one of his ancestors?

HOLDING AND DECISION: (Osborne, J.) No. One who adopts a spouse or other adult cannot thereby make the adoptee an heir to an estate created by an existing testamentary instrument executed by an ancestor of the adopter. It is clear that any adopted person, including an adult adoptee, may inherit from his adoptive parent. Moreover, the adoptee may ordinarily inherit, through an adoptive parent, the estate of an adoptive ancestor. In this case, it is probable that Amelia Minary intended her heirs to include any adopted children of her sons. Nonetheless, despite precedent to the contrary, a descendant should not be able to frustrate the declared intentions of an ancestor by adopting an adult for the sole purpose of making them an heir of the ancestor. Such a tactic, although permitted by the adoption laws, would thwart the ancestor's testamentary scheme. Therefore, the finding that Myra (P) is an heir of Amelia Minary must be reversed.

▶ *ANALYSIS*

Adoption is entirely a creature of statute and was not recognized in earliest common law times. Traditionally, an adopted child was entitled to inherit from, but not through, its adoptive parents. The modern statutory trend, however, is to permit the adoptee to inherit from the ancestors of its adoptive parents. Of course, once a legal adoption has been consummated, the adopted child loses all right to inherit from or through its natural parents.

■═■

Quicknotes

RESIDUARY ESTATE The portion of the estate remaining following distribution of the assets and the payment of costs.

■═■

O'Neal v. Wilkes

Virtual adoptee (P) v. Estate executor (D)

Ga. Sup. Ct., 263 Ga. 850, 439 S.E.2d 490 (1994).

NATURE OF CASE: Appeal from judgment n.o.v. denying equitable adoption claim.

FACT SUMMARY: O'Neal (P), who had been raised by testator but never formally adopted, petitioned the court for a declaration of virtual (equitable) adoption.

🏛 RULE OF LAW
A contract to adopt may not be specifically enforced unless the contract was entered into by a person with the legal authority to consent to the adoption.

FACTS: Hattie O'Neal's (P) mother died in 1957, when O'Neal (P) was eight years old. O'Neal's (P) father never recognized her as his daughter. After O'Neal (P) had lived with a maternal aunt for four years, she was taken to live with her paternal aunt, Page. Page ultimately sent O'Neal (P) to live with the testator. She lived with the testator for more than ten years, until she was married. The testator referred to O'Neal (P) as his daughter and her children as his grandchildren. After he died intestate, O'Neal (P) claimed she was entitled to inherit, under the theory of equitable adoption, the property she would have been entitled to had she been the testator's statutorily adopted daughter. Wilkes (D), the executor of the estate, contested O'Neal's (P) claim. The court granted a judgment n.o.v. in favor of Wilkes (D) on the grounds that Page, the paternal aunt who sent O'Neal (D) to live with the testator, had no legal authority to enter into an adoption contract with the testator. O'Neal (P) appealed.

ISSUE: May a contract to adopt be specifically enforced if it is entered into by a person without authority to consent to the adoption?

HOLDING AND DECISION: (Fletcher, J) No. A contract to adopt cannot be specifically enforced if it is entered into by a person without authority to consent to the adoption. Consent to an adoption may only be given by a child's parent or legal guardian. O'Neal's (P) Aunt Page was not O'Neal's (P) legal guardian; she was merely taking over a familial obligation in caring for the child. Because Page had no legal relationship with O'Neal (P), she could not consent to her adoption by the testator. The adoption contract was, therefore, invalid, and thus, O'Neal's (P) claim for an equitable adoption is defeated. Affirmed.

DISSENT: (Sears, J.) Equity treats as done that which ought to be done. By insisting that a person be appointed as a legal guardian before agreeing to a contract to adopt, the majority is harming the very person the requirement is designed to protect—the child.

▶ ANALYSIS

The majority does not grant the adoption in this case because the aunt was not the proper party to consent. The opinion, however, recognizes that O'Neal's (P) biological father also had no right to consent since he had abandoned her. The question the court fails to address is whether the child should be punished when there is no proper party to consent through no fault of her own. The result is anything but equitable toward the child.

■■■

Quicknotes

EQUITABLE ADOPTION An oral contract to adopt a child, not executed in accordance with statutory requirements, giving rise to rights of inheritance in the child upon the death of the promisor.

INTESTATE To die without leaving a valid testamentary instrument.

LEGAL CUSTODIAN Person having responsibility for a person or his property pursuant to law.

■■■

Woodward v. Commissioner of Social Security

Applicant for survivor benefits (P) v. Federal agency (D)

Mass. Sup. Jud. Ct., 435 Mass. 536, 760 N.E.2d 257 (2002).

NATURE OF CASE: Certified question regarding the inheritance rights of a child created through posthumous reproduction in an action for survivor benefits.

FACT SUMMARY: Woodward (P) sought survivor benefits for herself and her children, who were conceived using her deceased husband's previously preserved semen.

🏛 RULE OF LAW
A child resulting from posthumous reproduction may enjoy the inheritance rights of "issue" under the intestacy statute where there is a genetic relationship between the child and the decedent and the decedent consented to posthumous conception and to the support of any resulting child.

FACTS: Three years after the Woodwards were married, the husband was diagnosed with leukemia. The Woodwards subsequently arranged for a quantity of the husband's semen to be medically withdrawn and preserved in case he was left sterile after treatment. Shortly thereafter the husband died. Two years later, the wife (P) gave birth to twin girls conceived through artificial insemination using the husband's preserved semen. The Social Security Administration (SSA) (D) rejected the wife's (P) application for mother and child survivor benefits on the ground that she had not established that the twins were the husband's children within the meaning of the applicable law. While a series of appeals of the SSA (D) decision were pending, the Probate and Family Court entered a judgment of paternity and an order to amend both birth certificates declaring the deceased husband to be the children's father. A United States administrative law judge concluded that the children did not qualify for benefits because they were not entitled to inherit from the husband under the Massachusetts intestacy and paternity laws. The appeals counsel of the SSA (D) affirmed. The wife (P) appealed to the United States District Court for the District of Massachusetts seeking a declaratory judgment to reverse the commissioner's ruling and the United States District Court judge certified the question to this court.

ISSUE: If a married man and women arrange for sperm to be withdrawn from the husband for the purpose of artificially impregnating the wife, and the women is impregnated with that sperm after the man has died, will children resulting from such pregnancy enjoy the inheritance rights of natural children under the law of intestate succession?

HOLDING AND DECISION: (Marshall, C.J.) Yes. A child resulting from posthumous reproduction may enjoy the inheritance rights of "issue" under the intestacy statute where there is a genetic relationship between the child and the decedent and the decedent consented to posthumous conception and to the support of any resulting child. Although the intestacy statute does not limit the class of posthumous children to those in utero at the time of the decedent's death, posthumous reproduction may at times conflict with the purpose of the intestacy law and implicate other interests. This holding reconciles that conflict. The term "issue" means all genetic descendants and both marital and nonmarital descendants. Provisions of the intestacy statute regarding nonmarital children and posthumous children of an intestate are an expression of the legislature's intent to ensure that wealth passes from and to the actual family. The former requires that such a child must obtain a judicial determination that he is the father's child. Under our intestacy law, there is no reason that children conceived after the decedent's death, who are the decedent's direct genetic descendants, may not enjoy the same succession rights as children conceived before the decedent's death who are the decedent's direct genetic descendants. Massachusetts's interests in the best interests of the children, the orderly administration of estates and the reproductive rights of the genetic parents are balanced and harmonized by this holding to effect the legislature's over-all purposes. It can be assumed, based on precedent and public policy, that the legislature intended that posthumously conceived children be entitled to the same rights and protections of law, such as financial support from their parents, as children conceived before death. The protection of minor children has been a forefront issue in legislative action and jurisprudence. Despite the long existence of assistive reproductive technologies, the legislature has not acted to narrow the broad statutory class of posthumous children to restrict posthumously conceived children from taking in intestacy. According succession rights under our intestacy laws to posthumously conceived children will also not deteriorate the legislative purpose of providing certainty to heirs and creditors. The orderly, prompt, and accurate administration of intestate estates will not be affected. Since death ends a marriage, a posthumously conceived child is a nonmarital child. As such, our intestacy law mandates that a nonmarital

Continued on next page.

child must obtain a judicial determination of paternity as a prerequisite to succeeding to a portion of the father's intestate estate. Posthumous maternity is as uncertain until judicially established as is posthumous paternity, and neither more nor less difficult to prove. The final State interest implicated by this certified question is the reproductive rights of the genetic parent. Individuals have a protected right to control the use of their gametes. A decedent's silence, or his equivocal indications of a desire to parent posthumously, ought not to be construed as consent, but rather the prospective donor parent must clearly and unequivocally consent not only to posthumous reproduction but also to the support of any resulting child. That a man has medically preserved his gametes for use by his spouse may indicate only that he wished to reproduce after some contingency while he was alive, and not that he consented to the different circumstances of creating a child after his death. A rule that just required a genetic tie or the election to preserve gametes would thus be insufficient. In the present case, it is up to the wife (P) to prove that her husband consented to posthumously conceived children and that he consented to support such children.

ANALYSIS

This case demonstrates what effect modern technology is having on the definition of the family in the context of intestate succession. New Jersey has come out similarly to Massachusetts on this issue whereas Virginia and North Dakota have enacted the Uniform Status of Children of Assisted Conception Act (1988) which provides that a donor of an egg or sperm is not the parent of a child conceived through assisted conception. This case also brings up the yet-to-be-determined issue of the conflict between the State's interest in the orderly administration of estates effectuated by establishing a limitations period for the commencement of paternity claims, against the intestate estate and the burdens such limitations period imposes on the surviving parent and child.

Quicknotes

DECEDENT A person who is deceased.

INTESTATE To die without leaving a valid testamentary instrument.

INTESTATE SUCCESSION The scheme pursuant to which property is distributed in the absence of a valid will or of a disposition of particular property.

In re Estate of Mahoney

Widow (P) v. Decedent's parents (D)

Vt. Sup. Ct., 126 Vt. 31, 220 A.2d 475 (1966).

NATURE OF CASE: Appeal from an estate distribution order.

FACT SUMMARY: Mrs. Mahoney (P) was convicted of manslaughter for killing her husband.

🏛 RULE OF LAW
A conviction of voluntary manslaughter disables the party from taking under the decedent's will or through intestate succession.

FACTS: Mrs. Mahoney (P) was convicted of voluntary manslaughter for shooting her husband. Mr. Mahoney died intestate. His estate was ordered distributed to his mother (D) and father (D) since the probate court found that a conviction of voluntary manslaughter disabled Mrs. Mahoney (P) from taking any part of her husband's estate.

ISSUE: May a party convicted of the intentional killing of another inherit property from the decedent?

HOLDING AND DECISION: (Smith, J.) No. Conviction of murder or voluntary manslaughter disables the party convicted from inheriting any property from the decedent. Any inheritance in his favor is held as a constructive trust in favor of the other heirs or next of kin. While decisions in other jurisdictions vary with respect to voluntary manslaughter, the rule imposing a constructive trust appears to be the best solution. Although in this case there was no special finding concerning the voluntariness of Mrs. Mahoney's (P) actions, the court obviously concluded that she had been convicted of the felonious killing of her husband. While a constructive trust could be imposed on the bequest, the probate court could only apply the laws of distribution and descent and incorrectly awarded the property directly to Mr. Mahoney's parents (D). We must reverse and remand for a constructive trust action to be brought in a proper court of chancery.

▶ ANALYSIS

In a majority of states, a killer is barred by statute from inheriting any interest in the estate of his victim. In jurisdictions where no such statute has been enacted, courts have shown a reluctance to impose any restraints on the killer's right to inherit. Sometimes, however, a court of equity will adopt the constructive trust approach favored by the Mahoney court, although the trust device seems to unduly complicate the nature of the relief granted. Note that at earliest common law, the commission of any felony, not only murder, deprived the wrongdoer of his right to inherit property.

Quicknotes

CONSTRUCTIVE TRUST   A trust that arises by operation of law whereby the court imposes a trust upon property lawfully held by one party for the benefit of another, as a result of some wrongdoing by the party in possession so as to avoid unjust enrichment.

RESIDUE   That property which remains following the distribution of the assets of the testator's estate.

Troy v. Hart

Representative (P) v. Estate representative (D)

Md. Ct. Spec. App., 697 A.2d 113 (1997).

NATURE OF CASE: Appeal from denial of rescission of inheritance disclaimer.

FACT SUMMARY: Lettich's representative, Troy (P), disclaimed an inheritance interest available to his client but did not report the situation to Medicaid.

RULE OF LAW

Persons who disclaim an inheritance must still report the potential change in financial status when enrolled in means-tested government programs.

FACTS: Lettich required care at a hospice and appointed Troy (P) as his attorney and representative. When Lettich's financial resources were exhausted, Troy (P) was able to obtain Medicaid assistance for him. Soon after, Lettich's sister died intestate with a $300,000 estate. Hart (D), also Lettich's sister and the estate's representative, met with Lettich and assisted him in executing a disclaimer of his interest but did not tell Troy (P) or Medicaid officials. Troy (P) then filed suit to rescind the disclaimer and remove Hart (D) as representative of the estate. The trial court ruled for Hart (D) and Troy (P) appealed.

ISSUE: Must persons who disclaim an inheritance report the potential change in financial status when enrolled in means-tested government programs?

HOLDING AND DECISION: (Thieme, J.) Yes. Persons who disclaim an inheritance must still report the potential change in financial status when enrolled in means-tested government programs. Eligibility for Medicaid depends on meeting various income and resources tests. Eligibility status can change if a recipient's financial circumstances change, so the law requires notice within 10 days. If one fails to disclose a change, the shadow of fraud surfaces. If a Medicaid recipient renounces an inheritance that would cause him to be financially disqualified from benefits, Medicaid is entitled to recover payments made on the potential inheritor's behalf. In the present case, Lettich's disclaimer must still be valid, but the interests of the surviving sisters, Hart (D) and McLaughlin, are subject to the claims that Medicaid has for paying for Lettich's care following the renunciation. Affirmed.

▶ ANALYSIS

The court used the doctrine of unjust enrichment to find that Hart (D) and her other sister were not entitled to the full amount of the inheritance. The court found that the inheritance was subject to Medicaid's constructive trust. A Wisconsin court has held that Medicaid eligibility can be terminated when a surviving spouse does not elect a forced share of an estate.

Quicknotes

UNJUST ENRICHMENT Principle that one should not be unjustly enriched at the expense of another

Wills: Capacity and Contests

Quick Reference Rules of Law

In re Estate of Wright

Parties not identified.

Cal. Sup. Ct., 7 Cal. 2d 348, 60 P.2d 434 (1936).

NATURE OF CASE: Appeal from denial of admission of will to probate on testamentary incapacity grounds.

FACT SUMMARY: The executrix of Wright's estate argued that testimony, by witnesses to the will and others, that Wright was of unsound mind when he executed his will, was insufficient to support testamentary incapacity because the opinions on which that testimony rested was based on trivialities relating to foibles, idiosyncrasies, moral or mental irregularities, or departures from the normal.

🏛 **RULE OF LAW**
Evidence of mere foibles, idiosyncrasies, moral or mental irregularities, or departures from the normal is insufficient to support a case of testamentary incapacity where they do not relate directly to the testamentary act.

FACTS: Wright was 69 when he died. He executed his will one year and four months before his death. He went alone to the office of Thomas, a notary public and realtor with whom he had transacted business and whom he had known for many years, bringing with him memoranda sheets upon which he had written the names of the persons whom he wished to enjoy his property and the specific shares thereof after his death. Thomas prepared the will accordingly. Wright gave his daughter one piece of improved real property. He gave a friend another piece of property. To his granddaughter he bequeathed his undivided interest in an estate, and he named seven others to whom he made nominal bequests of $1 each. The daughter contested the will, claiming her father did not have the requisite testamentary capacity when he executed the will. Thomas and the other witnesses to the will testified that they believed Wright had been of unsound mind when they witnessed him. Others also testified they thought he was of unsound mind. The testimony was in the form of opinions that, inter alia, the will was unusual in that it left $1 gifts, that he drank and was drunk much of the time, that he was queer, that he frightened children, that he hid things around the house, that he would play mean pranks, and that he exhibited other unusual behavior on occasion. There was no evidence that he was medically insane. The probate court denied the admission of Wright's will to probate on the basis of this evidence. The California Supreme Court granted review.

ISSUE: Is evidence of mere foibles, idiosyncrasies, moral or mental irregularities, or departures from the normal insufficient to support a case of testamentary incapacity where they do not relate directly to the testamentary act?

HOLDING AND DECISION: (Seawell, J.) Yes. Evidence of mere foibles, idiosyncrasies, moral or mental irregularities, or departures from the normal is insufficient to support a case of testamentary incapacity where they do not relate directly to the testamentary act. Taking all the evidence adduced by the daughter (contestant) as true, it falls far below the requirements of the law as constituting satisfactory rebuttal of the inference of testamentary capacity. No proof whatever was offered tending to rebut the testator's ability to transact or conduct his business or to care for himself except in a few cases of illness brought about by natural causes or excesses or by accident. To a great extent the grounds upon which the witnesses base their opinions are mere trivialities. As to the testimony of the drafter of the will and the other witnesses thereto, who afterwards attempted to repudiate all they had done, such testimony is suspect or "simply worthless." This is because the legal presumption is always in favor of sanity, especially after attestation by subscribing witnesses, because it is the duty of the subscribing witnesses to be satisfied of the testator's sanity before they subscribe the instrument. There was no evidence that Wright suffered from settled insanity, hallucinations, or delusions. Testamentary capacity cannot be destroyed by showing a few isolated acts, foibles, idiosyncrasies, moral or mental irregularities, or departures from the normal unless they directly bear upon and have influenced the testamentary act. No medical testimony as to the extent of any injury the testator had received or its effect upon him either physically or mentally was introduced in the case. The burden was upon the daughter throughout the case, and she failed to meet that burden. In fact, the evidence tended to show that Wright appreciated his relations and obligations to others (e.g., giving his daughter a house) and that he was mindful of the property that he possessed. Reversed.

Continued on next page.

▶ *ANALYSIS*

Under the Restatement (Third) of Property, the requirements for mental capacity are minimal: the testator must be an adult, must be capable of knowing and understanding in a general way the nature and extent of his or her property, the natural objects of his or her bounty, and the disposition that he or she is making of that property. The testator must also be capable of relating these elements to one another and forming an orderly desire regarding the disposition of the property. It seems that Wright satisfied all of these criteria.

■━━■

Quicknotes

EXECUTRIX A female person designated by a deceased individual to effectuate the disposition of his property pursuant to a testamentary instrument.

TESTAMENTARY INCAPACITY Absence of the requisite level of mental capacity required by law at the time a testator executes a testamentary instrument in order for the document to be valid.

■━━■

In re Strittmater

Cousins of decedent (P) v. Court (D)

N.J. Ct. Err. & App., 140 N.J. Eq. 94, 53 A.2d 205 (1947).

NATURE OF CASE: Appeal from decree admitting will to probate.

FACT SUMMARY: Strittmater left her estate to the National Women's Party out of an extreme hatred for men.

RULE OF LAW
If a will is a product of an insane delusion, it will not be probated.

FACTS: Strittmater, upon her death, bequeathed her estate to the National Women's Party rather than to her cousins with whom she had very little to do. The cousins (P) contested the will. Strittmater's personal physician testified that she felt Strittmater had suffered from schizophrenia all her adult life. Strittmater's mental illness was manifested by her angry comments about her deceased parents; her vocal, intense hatred of men; and her fervent support of the women's movement. However, her relationships with her bankers and lawyer were entirely normal. The orphans court admitted the will to probate, the cousins (P) appealed and the probate was set aside.

ISSUE: Will a will that is the product of an insane delusion be probated?

HOLDING AND DECISION: (Per curiam) No. A will that is the product of an insane delusion will not be probated. The testator must have been sane at the time of the will's execution to enforce the will. Strittmater's extreme hatred of men and "feminism to a neurotic extreme" demonstrated her obvious mental illness. This is true even though she had the capacity to transact ordinary business. While Strittmater gave her money to this organization, to which she belonged for eleven years, she did not involve herself enough in the party to justify her bequest. Strittmater's will was the result of mental illness and, thus, will not be entered into probate. Affirmed.

ANALYSIS

There are three historical rationales for the sanity requirement. First of all, wills should carry out a person's intent; if the will is a product of insanity, it cannot represent his wishes. Secondly, an insane person is not a "person" as a recognized legal entity and therefore cannot be allowed to bequeath possessions. Thirdly, mental capacity is required in order to protect the family, which relies on the decedent for economic support.

Quicknotes

PROBATE The administration of a decedent's estate.

TESTATRIX A woman who dies having drafted and executed a will or testament.

In re Honigman

Wife of decedent (P) v. Court (D)

N.Y. Ct. App., 8 N.Y.2d 244 (1960).

NATURE OF CASE: Appeal from the denial of probate of a will.

FACT SUMMARY: Honigman had an unfounded delusion that his wife was unfaithful to him.

RULE OF LAW

A person suffering from an insane delusion as to one of his heirs has no capacity to make a will with respect to that person.

FACTS: After forty years of a reasonably happy marriage, Honigman, after a serious operation, began to believe that his wife (P) was unfaithful to him. Honigman began accusing her of all sorts of unreasonable acts, including hiding men in the cellar and closets, having them climb up bed sheets to reach their apartment, etc. Honigman visited a psychiatrist and several times mentioned to witnesses that he was mentally ill. Honigman died, leaving a small life estate to his wife (P), the remainder to his relatives. His attorney stated that his decision to make a new will just before his death was based on the belief of his wife's infidelity, her large independent estate, and the need of his other relatives. Mrs. Honigman (P) moved to deny probate of the will, alleging that, as to her, Mr. Honigman was operating under an insane delusion and lacked the mental capacity to make a will. While some testimony was offered to establish some slight grounds for Mr. Honigman's belief, the jury found that he lacked mental capacity to make a will with respect to Mrs. Honigman (P), though he was sane in all other respects. On appeal, the judgment was reversed, and probate was ordered.

ISSUE: May a will be denied probate where the testator had an insane delusion concerning one of his heirs, though he was sane in all other respects?

HOLDING AND DECISION: (Dye, J.) Yes. A will may be denied probate if the testator lacked the mental capacity to make a will. Probate may also be denied if testator was acting under an insane delusion with respect to one of the natural objects of his bounty, here his wife (P) of forty years. The jury was warranted in finding that there was no rational or reasonable proof of infidelity and that Honigman was operating under a totally insane delusion as to his wife's conduct. It could have also found that the new will was a product of his delusion. It is immaterial that testator could have had other reasons for his actions. It is sufficient that the dispositive provisions of the will might have been caused by the in-sane delusion. The court erred in admitting the testimony of Mrs. Honigman (P) and may have erred in excluding the testimony of a priest from whom Mr. Honigman sought advice. A new trial is ordered.

DISSENT: (Fuld, J.) It is not enough to show that suspicions are groundless, unwarranted, or even foolish. Testator must be shown to be insane as to that person. The evidence herein fails to establish insanity. The judgment directing probate should be affirmed.

ANALYSIS

In *Dixon v. Webster*, 551 S.W.2d 888 (1977), the court stated that to establish an insane delusion more was required than a showing that testator was operating under a fixed, incorrect belief. It was also necessary to establish that testator retained the belief against all arguments raised to disprove it.

Quicknotes

LEGATEE A person who is granted a legacy or bequest pursuant to a will.

PROBATE The administration of a decedent's estate.

TESTAMENTARY INCAPACITY Absence of the requisite level of mental capacity required by law, at the time a testator executes a testamentary instrument, in order for the document to be valid.

Lipper v. Weslow

Son of decedent (D) v. Disinherited grandchildren of decedent (P)

Tex. Ct. Civ. App., 369 S.W.2d 698 (1963).

NATURE OF CASE: Appeal from refusal to admit will to probate.

FACT SUMMARY: The will of a testatrix was refused probate on the basis that it had been procured by undue influence of her son (D), who was also the lawyer who had prepared the document. The challenge was brought by three grandchildren (P) of the testatrix who had been specifically disinherited by the terms of the will.

🏛 RULE OF LAW
Undue influence is shown when such control was exercised over the mind of the testator so as to overcome his free agency and free will and to substitute the will of another so as to cause the testator to do what he would not otherwise have done but for such control.

FACTS: Shortly before her death, Mrs. Block executed a will that in large measure left her estate to her two surviving children. The will specifically disinherited three of her grandchildren (P) who were descendants of a son who had died some years before. The will contained a lengthy explanation of her reasons for excluding the grandchildren (P). The basic theme of this portion of the will was that the grandchildren's mother had been unfriendly toward the testatrix and that the grandchildren (P) themselves had shown no interest in the testatrix and had refrained from any contact with her. The will had been prepared by the testatrix's son (D), who was also a lawyer and had maintained close ties with his mother. The disinheritance of the grandchildren (P) had the effect of increasing his share of the estate by redistributing that portion that would otherwise have gone to the grandchildren (P). The grandchildren [the Weslows (P)] challenged the admission of the will to probate, contending that it had been procured through the undue influence of Lipper (D), the lawyer-son. The Weslows (P) contended the disinheritance clause had been inserted because Lipper (D) disliked his deceased brother. Further, the Weslows (P) disputed the factual assertions in the will that they had neglected their grandmother and contended that their attempts at contact with her had somehow been thwarted by Lipper (D). A jury returned a verdict that the will had been procured by undue influence, and the will was refused probate. Lipper (D) then brought this appeal, contending the verdict did not have a factual basis.

ISSUE: Is undue influence shown when such control was exercised over the mind of the testator as to overcome his free agency and free will and to substitute the will of another so as to cause the testator to do what he would otherwise have done but for such control?

HOLDING AND DECISION: (McDonald, C.J.) Yes. The evidence produced at trial showed that although the testatrix was 81 years old at the time this will was executed, she was sound both physically and mentally. The Weslows (P) were able to show opportunity and motive for Lipper (D) to exercise influence over the testatrix in the preparation of her will. There was a factual dispute over whether the recitation of neglect by the Weslows (P) was a true picture of what actually occurred. However, a showing of undue influence requires more than circumstantial evidence of opportunity and motive. There must be a positive showing that such control was exercised over the mind of the testator as to overcome his free will and free agency and to substitute the will of another so as to cause the testator to do what he would not otherwise have done but for such control, the groundwork for such confidential relationship and motive in the form of an unilateral disposition of the testator's estate. But thereafter, the party contending that undue influence existed must bear the burden of proof that the will of the testator was replaced by that of another. The Weslows (P) laid the groundwork but failed to carry the burden of proof thereafter required. The absence of the required proof of actual influence is sufficient to warrant a reversal of the judgment below.

▶ ANALYSIS

A principle ignored by the appellate court was that any bequest to the attorney preparing the will is presumed to have resulted from undue influence. The ABA Model Rules of Professional Conduct strongly recommends that where a client wishes to name his attorney as a beneficiary, the attorney should refer the client to another disinterested attorney for preparation of the will. The clause in the will outlining the reasons for the exclusion of the grandchildren would seem to be entitled to little weight in determining the issue of undue influence. If the will was induced by such influence, then this clause would have been no more valid than any other portion and would become merely a self-serving attempt by the influencer to cover his acts.

■━■

Continued on next page.

Quicknotes

PROBATE The administration of a decedent's estate.

TESTATRIX A woman who dies having drafted and executed a will or testament.

UNDUE INFLUENCE Improper influence that deprives the individual freedom of choice or substitutes another's choice for the person's own choice.

■═■

In re Will of Moses

Sister of decedent (P) v. Decedent's beneficiary (D)

Miss. Sup. Ct., 227 So. 2d 829 (1969).

NATURE OF CASE: Appeal from denial of probate.

FACT SUMMARY: The fact that an independent attorney was consulted and drew up the will by which Fannie Taylor Moses left most of her property to her attorney/lover did not overcome the presumption of undue influence, according to the court that denied probate.

🏛 RULE OF LAW
A presumption of undue influence arises when an attorney with whom the testator had a continuing fiduciary relationship is a beneficiary under the will, which is not necessarily overcome simply because the will was actually drawn up by an independent attorney with whom the testator consulted on his or her own.

FACTS: The thrice-married Fannie Taylor Moses had an ongoing affair with an attorney, Holland (D), who was fifteen years her junior. She suffered from heart trouble, had a breast removed due to cancer, and was an alcoholic during the term of their affair. Her elder sister (P) attacked Fannie Taylor Moses' will on the grounds of undue influence by Holland (D). The evidence showed that Moses had sought the advice of an attorney on her own, that he had no knowledge or connection with Holland (D), and that he drafted a will to accomplish what Moses had said was her wish, i.e., to leave her estate to Holland (D). The chancellor found undue influence and denied probate. Holland (D) appealed.

ISSUE: Is the presumption of undue influence that arises when an attorney with whom the testator had a fiduciary relationship necessarily overcome by showing that the testator sought the advice of and had an independent attorney actually draw up the will?

HOLDING AND DECISION: (Smith, J.) No. The existence of a continuing fiduciary relationship between a testator and an attorney-beneficiary itself gives rise to a presumption of undue influence. While that presumption can be overcome, the mere fact that an independent attorney acted as a scrivener in properly putting into will form what Mrs. Moses wanted will not overcome the presumption of undue influence that exists in this case. There was no meaningful independent advice or counsel touching upon the proposed testamentary disposition to a nonrelative in exclusion of her blood relatives. Affirmed.

DISSENT: (Robertson, J.) If full knowledge, deliberate and voluntary action, and independent consent and advice have not been proved in this case, then they just cannot be proved.

▶ ANALYSIS

Disbarment was the price that was paid by John D. Randall, president of the American Bar Association in 1959–60, for naming himself as beneficiary of a client's $4.5-million estate. Another area in which undue influence has played an important role is the challenging of wills bequeathing estates to the surviving partner in a homosexual relationship.

■═■

Quicknotes

FIDUCIARY RELATIONSHIP Person holding a legal obligation to act for the benefit of another.

PROBATE The administration of a decedent's estate.

UNDUE INFLUENCE Improper influence that deprives the individual freedom of choice or substitutes another's choice for the person's own choice.

■═■

Latham v. Father Divine

Cousins of decedent (P) v. Beneficiary (D)

N.Y. Ct. App., 299 N.Y. 22, 85 N.E.2d 168, 11 A.L.R.2d 802 (1949).

NATURE OF CASE: Suit in equity to impose constructive trust on proceeds from a will.

FACT SUMMARY: The natural heirs of a testatrix sought to gain control of a will distribution made to a religious leader who had been named sole beneficiary. The heirs claimed that the testatrix had been prevented from executing a new will in their favor by the fraud and undue influence of the religious leader.

🏛 RULE OF LAW
Where a testator is prevented from executing a new will in favor of an intended beneficiary by the fraud, duress, or undue influence of a present beneficiary or heir, the property intended to go to the new beneficiary will pass to the present beneficiary subject to a constructive trust in favor of the intended beneficiary.

FACTS: Mary Lyon died, leaving a will which devised her entire estate to Father Divine (D), the leader of a religious cult, and to two corporations controlled by him. The will was accepted for probate after a contest filed by two first cousins (P) of the testatrix. Thereafter, the cousins (Latham [P]), who were the testatrix's only close relatives, instituted this suit, claiming that the testatrix had expressed an intention to alter her will so as to bequeath to them property in the amount of $350,000. Latham (P) further alleged that the testatrix had been prevented from doing so by the false representations, undue influence, and physical force of Father Divine (D). Latham (P) requested that a constructive trust in the cousins' favor be imposed on the proceeds of the will to the extent of the property that would otherwise have gone to them if the testatrix had not been prevented from executing the new will. The suit was dismissed for failure to state a cause of action, and Latham (P) appealed that dismissal.

ISSUE: Where a testator is prevented from executing a new will in favor of an intended beneficiary by the fraud, duress, or undue influence of a present beneficiary or heir, will the property intended to go to the new beneficiary pass to the present beneficiary subject to a constructive trust in favor of the intended beneficiary?

HOLDING AND DECISION: (Desmond, J.) Yes. In reviewing an appeal of a dismissal of a complaint for insufficiency, the allegations of that complaint must be taken as true. If, on that basis, the complaint fails to state a cause of action, then the dismissal must be affirmed. Therefore, we must as-

sume that the allegations of fraud, undue influence, and physical coercion actually occurred. Father Divine (D) states that a showing of the alleged acts cannot empower a court to write a new will for the testatrix. In this contention he is correct. But, where a testator is prevented from executing a new will by the wrongful acts of a present beneficiary or heir to the detriment of an intended beneficiary, and the existing will is otherwise valid, then the existing beneficiary takes his bequest subject to a constructive trust as to that portion that would have gone to the intended beneficiary but for the wrongful acts. A court of equity attempts, to the extent possible, to render complete justice. By imposing a constructive trust to avoid the result of the wrongful prevention of the execution of a new will, the court does not violate the Statute of Frauds or ignore the requirements for a valid will. The will itself is not affected; it is only the property passed under that will. If Latham (P) is able to show that the testatrix intended a different testamentary disposition than is reflected in the probated will, then Father Divine (D) cannot profit by his misconduct. The dismissal is reversed with instructions for a trial on the merits.

▶ *ANALYSIS*

The constructive trust remedy has also been applied where an impatient beneficiary has killed the testator in order to advance the date of the inheritance. In one instance, a number of beneficiaries were named in a will. The testatrix expressed a desire to change her will, substantially cutting out the presently named beneficiaries. Some of the present beneficiaries succeeded in physically preventing the testatrix from executing the newly drawn will. The result was a trust imposed on the entire proceeds of the will, even though this disinherited some beneficiaries who did not participate in the wrongful acts. The court reasoned that had the testatrix' intent not been thwarted, even the innocent beneficiaries would have lost their bequests. They should not be allowed to profit unjustly by the wrongful acts of the others.

▬▬▬

Continued on next page.

Quicknotes

CONSTRUCTIVE TRUST A trust that arises by operation of law whereby the court imposes a trust upon property lawfully held by one party for the benefit of another, as a result of some wrongdoing by the party in possession so as to avoid unjust enrichment.

DURESS Unlawful threats or other coercive behavior by one person that causes another to commit acts that he would not otherwise do.

FRAUD A false representation of facts with the intent that another will rely on the misrepresentation to his detriment.

LEGATEE A person who is granted a legacy or bequest pursuant to a will.

UNJUST ENRICHMENT The unlawful acquisition of money or property of another for which both law and equity require restitution to be made.

Wills: Formalities and Forms

Quick Reference Rules of Law

Stevens v. Casdorph

Decedent's niece (P) v. Beneficiary (D)

W. Va. Sup. Ct. App., 203 W. Va. 450, 508 S.E.2d 610 (1998)

NATURE OF THE CASE: Appeal from grant of summary judgment denying action to set aside will.

FACT SUMMARY: The testator was not in the presence of the witnesses when he signed his will and the witnesses were not in the presence of each other when they signed as subscribing witnesses to his will. The Stevenses (P) sought to have the will set aside claiming it had not been properly executed.

> ### 🏛 RULE OF LAW
> To be valid, a will must have been signed by the testator in the presence of two competent witnesses who then must sign the will in the presence of the testator and each other.

FACTS: Miller, the testator, was brought to a bank by the Casdorphs (D) to execute his will. Miller was elderly and confined to a wheelchair. After Miller had signed his will, Pauley, a bank employee and a notary, brought it to two other bank employees who each signed the will as witnesses. Neither of the bank employees witnessed Miller signing the will. Miller did not see either bank employee sign the will and neither bank employee saw the other sign the will, although all were in the lobby of the bank. Miller did not acknowledge his signature on the will to either of the bank employees who had signed his will and neither employee acknowledged her signature on the will to Miller or to each other. When Miller died, he left most of his estate to the Casdorphs (D). The Stevenses (P), nieces of Miller, filed suit to have the will set aside, asserting that it was invalid because it had been improperly executed. Both parties moved for summary judgment. The Stevenses' (P) motion for summary judgment was denied by the circuit court, but the Casdorphs' motion for summary judgment was granted. The Stevenses appealed.

ISSUE: Must a will be signed by the testator in the presence of two witnesses and then signed by each witness in the testator's presence and in the presence of each in order to be validly executed?

HOLDING AND DECISION: (Per curiam) Yes. A will is not validly executed unless the testator has signed it in the presence of two competent witnesses who then must sign the will in the presence of the testator and each other. Under a narrow exception in West Virginia, a will is still valid if a witness acknowledges her signature on the will in the physical presence of both the testator and the other subscribing witness.

The facts in this case do not fit into this narrow exception. The testator did not sign in the presence of either witness. Neither witness signed in the presence of the testator or in the presence of each other. Neither witness acknowledged her signature on the will in the testator's presence or the other subscribing witness. Hence the will was not properly executed. Since the will was not properly executed, it is invalid. Reversed.

DISSENT: (Workman, J.) Inflexible, technical applications of statutory requirements that a testator must be "in the presence" of the subscribing witnesses when he signs his will and that they in turn must sign in the presence of the testator and each other lead to inequitable results. The intention of the statute is to prevent fraud. Where there is no claim of fraud, incapacity, or undue influence, a will is valid if there has been substantial compliance with the statute.

▌ ANALYSIS

Not all courts interpret "in the presence of" requirement as stringently as this court did. Many jurisdictions employ the "line-of-vision" test. To meet this test, the testator must have been able to see the witness signing without adjusting his position. He need not have actually seen the witness sign the will. Other jurisdictions use the "conscious-presence" test. Under this test the testator need only sense the presence of the witnesses as they sign. The Restatement 3d of Property Section 3.1, comment p, also takes the "conscious presence" approach. The current Uniform Probate Code does not have a "presence" requirement except for when a testator asks another person to sign for him. The person signing for the testator must sign "in the testator's conscious presence."

Quicknotes

TESTATOR One who executes a will.

Estate of Parsons

Parties not identified.

Cal. Ct. App., 103 Cal. App. 3d 384 (1980).

NATURE OF CASE: Appeal in a probate proceeding.

FACT SUMMARY: Of primary concern during the probate of Geneve Parsons's will was whether or not a subscribing witness to the will could be considered to have been a "disinterested" witness by reason of her subsequent disclaimer of a bequest made therein to her.

🏛 RULE OF LAW
A subscribing witness to a will who is named in the will as a beneficiary does not become a "disinterested" subscribing witness by filing a disclaimer of his interest after the testator's death.

FACTS: Two of the three persons who signed Geneve Parsons's will as attesting witnesses were named therein as beneficiaries. After the testator's death, Nielson filed a disclaimer of her $100 bequest. Relatives of Parsons claimed an interest in the estate on the ground that the devise of certain real property to Gower, the other subscribing witness to whom a bequest was made, was invalid. The basis for this claim was a statute which provided that a gift to a subscribing witness is void "unless there are two other and disinterested subscribing witnesses to the will." The relatives insisted that Nielson's subsequent disclaimer of her bequest did not change the fact that she was not a "disinterested" subscribing witness, that only one of the subscribing witnesses could, thus, be considered "disinterested," and that the property bequest to Gower was consequently invalid. The trial court rejected that argument.

ISSUE: Does a subscribing witness to a will who is named as a beneficiary therein become "disinterested" by filing a disclaimer of his interest after the testator's death?

HOLDING AND DECISION: (Grodin, J.) No. While the court might like to substitute a rule more to its liking, the fact is that a subscribing witness to a will who is named as a beneficiary therein does not become a "disinterested" subscribing witness by filing a disclaimer of his interest after the testator's death. The statutory provision regarding subscribing witnesses looks solely to the time of execution and attestation of the will. So, it follows that a subsequent disclaimer will be ineffective to transform an interested witness into a "disinterested" one. If such a transformation were possible, the purpose of the subscribing witness statute, as it was designed, would be undermined, i.e. to protect the testator from fraud and undue influence at the very moment when he executes his will. Reversed.

▶ ANALYSIS

Uniform Probate Code § 2-505 adopts the following rule: "(a) Any person generally competent to be a witness may act as a witness to a will. (b) A will or any provision thereof is not invalid because the will is signed by an interested witness." Solicitation of business by the attorney-drafter of a will in regard to his being employed as the estate's attorney is a violation of the code of professional responsibility. *State v. Gulbankian*, 196 N.W.2d 733 (Wis. 1972).

Quicknotes

FRAUD A false representation of facts with the intent that another will rely on the misrepresentation to his detriment.

PROBATE The administration of a decedent's estate.

SUBSCRIBING WITNESS A person who witnesses the execution of a document and signs his name thereto.

UNDUE INFLUENCE Improper influence that deprives the individual freedom of choice or substitutes another's choice for the person's own choice.

In re Pavlinko's Estate

Residuary (P) v. Register of wills (D)

Pa. Sup. Ct., 394 Pa. 564, 148 A.2d 528 (1959).

NATURE OF CASE: Action to have a will admitted to probate.

FACT SUMMARY: Vasil and Hellen Pavlinko inadvertently signed one another's wills. On Vasil's death, Martin (P), a legatee under Hellen's will, sought to have that will probated as Vasil's.

🏛 RULE OF LAW
A court may not rewrite a clear and unambiguous will even for the purpose of implementing the obvious intentions of the testator.

FACTS: Vasil and Hellen Pavlinko, neither of whom spoke much English, had wills prepared for them. Both left their property to the other, and both designated Elias Martin (P), Hellen's brother, as residuary. Through inadvertence, Hellen Pavlinko signed the will that had been prepared for her husband, and he signed the will that had been prepared for her. Several years later, Hellen Pavlinko died. Some time afterward, her husband also passed away. Upon Vasil's death, Martin (P) filed Hellen's will, the only one that Vasil had signed, and asked that it be admitted to probate as Vasil's will. The will was denied probate, and the court affirmed. Martin (P) appealed.

ISSUE: If a party mistakenly signs another will instead of his own, may the will he signed be modified at his death to include the provisions of the instrument which he had intended to sign?

HOLDING AND DECISION: (Bell, J.) No. A court may not rewrite a clear and unambiguous will even for the purpose of implementing the obvious intentions of the testator. The will that Vasil Pavlinko signed leaves the entire estate to him. In order to award the property to Martin (P) as residuary legatee, it would be necessary to rewrite virtually the entire instrument, and such a procedure cannot be countenanced in the case of a will so totally lacking in ambiguity as this one. Thus, the will that Vasil signed cannot be admitted to probate as his will. The will that was prepared for him cannot, of course, be probated, because he never signed it. Therefore, the regrettable result, which is supported by the holding of a case that presented a fact situation substantially the same as that of this case, is that Martin (P) is entitled to no relief.

DISSENT: (Musmanno, J.) The will signed by Vasil Pavlinko should be admitted to probate. Even if it is not possible to give effect to every provision of that will, there is no reason why the court cannot enforce the residuary clause, which designates Martin (P) as beneficiary.

▶ ANALYSIS

This case illustrates the reluctance of courts to compromise the prophylactic objects of statutes relating to the formal execution of wills. The court declined to "bend the rules" and, thus, permitted the statute to operate as an intent-defeating device. At least one court, albeit a distant one, granted relief in a case similar to *In re Pavlinko's Estate*. In *Guardian Trust & Executors Co. of New Zealand Ltd.. v. Inwood*, (1946) N.Z.L.R. 614, wills were prepared for two sisters, each of whom left their estates to the other. Jane then signed Maude's will, but a New Zealand court enforced that will after striking the word "Jane" from the body of the will.

▬▬▬

Quicknotes

PROBATE The administration of a decedent's estate.

RESIDUARY LEGATEE The recipient of the residuary estate of a testator.

▬▬▬

In re Snide

Parties not identified.

N.Y. Ct. App., 52 N.Y.2d 193, 418 N.E.2d 656, 437 N.Y.S.2d 63 (1981).

NATURE OF CASE: Appeal from reversal of decree admitting will to probate.

FACT SUMMARY: Snide, decedent, and his wife, Rose, intending to execute mutual wills at a common execution ceremony, each executed by mistake the will intended for the other. Rose argued that the will signed by Snide was admissible as reformed to substitute Snide's name (Harvey) for Rose's and vice versa.

🏛 RULE OF LAW

Where a husband and wife execute identical wills at the same time, but by mistake they each sign the other's will, upon death of one of the spouses, the will that the decedent spouse actually signed is admissible to probate provided the significance of the only variance between the two instruments is fully explained, the will is genuine, and the will was executed in accordance with law.

FACTS: Harvey Snide, decedent, and his wife Rose, intending to execute mutual wills at a common execution ceremony, each executed by mistake the will intended for the other. All the required formalities of execution were followed, and there was no question of the decedent's testamentary capacity or intention and of his belief that he was signing his last will and testament. Except for obvious differences in the names of the donors and beneficiaries on the wills, they were in all respects identical. Rose offered the instrument that her husband actually signed for probate. The guardian ad litem representing Snide's infant child objected, because denial of probate was the only way in which the minor child would receive a present share of the estate. The guardian ad litem argued that the will was inadmissible because Snide lacked the requisite testamentary intent. The surrogate court decreed that it could be admitted, and further, that it could be reformed to substitute the name "Harvey" wherever the name "Rose" appeared and the name "Rose" wherever the name "Harvey" appeared. The appellate court reversed, on the law, holding that such an instrument may not be admitted to probate, and the state's highest court granted review.

ISSUE: Where a husband and wife execute identical wills at the same time, but by mistake they each sign the other's will, upon death of one of the spouses, is the will that the decedent spouse actually signed admissible to probate provided the significance of the only variance between the two instruments is

fully explained, the will is genuine, and the will was executed in accordance with law?

HOLDING AND DECISION: (Wachtler, J.) Yes. Where a husband and wife execute identical wills at the same time, but by mistake they each sign the other's will, upon death of one of the spouses, the will that the decedent spouse actually signed is admissible to probate provided the significance of the only variance between the two instruments is fully explained, the will is genuine, and the will was executed in accordance with law. The gist of the guardian ad litem's argument is that Snide lacked the required testamentary intent because he never intended to execute the document he actually signed. However, a formalistic approach, holding that this intent attaches irrevocably to the document prepared, rather than the testamentary scheme it reflects, is rejected. Here, although Snide mistakenly signed the will prepared for his wife, it is significant that the dispositive provisions in both wills, except for the names, were identical.

Moreover, the significance of the only variance between the two instruments is fully explained by consideration of the documents together, as well as in the undisputed surrounding circumstances. Under such facts it would indeed be ironic—if not perverse—to state that because what has occurred is so obvious, and what was intended so clear, we must act to nullify rather than sustain this testamentary scheme. The instrument in question was undoubtedly genuine, and it was executed in the manner required by the statute. Under these unique circumstances, it was properly admitted to probate. Reversed and remitted.

DISSENT: (Jones, J.) Various jurisdictions have split on whether to admit a will under circumstances identical to the ones presented in this case. Some, while expressing regret at having to do so, have applied the traditional doctrines. Others, as the majority, have been moved by the transparency of the obvious error and the egregious frustration of undisputed intention that would ensue from failure to correct that error. In this case, precedent should be adhered to.

Continued on next page.

▶ *ANALYSIS*

Under the Uniform Probate Code, this case could be treated as one of harmless error. Section 2-503 of the Code provides that although a document or writing has not been executed in accordance with the Code, the document or writing is treated as if it had been executed properly if it is established by clear and convincing evidence that the decedent intended the document or writing to constitute the decedent's will or other testamentary document.

■═■

Quicknotes

DECEDENT A person who is deceased.

HARMLESS ERROR An error taking place during trial that does not require the reviewing court to overturn or modify the trial court's judgment in that it did not affect the appellant's substantial rights or the disposition of the action.

■═■

In re Will of Ranney

Parties not identified.

N.J. Sup. Ct., 124 N.J. 1, 589 A.2d 1339 (1991).

NATURE OF CASE: Appeal from reversal of a ruling in a will contest denying admission to probate.

FACT SUMMARY: After Ranney's death, his wife, Betty, contested probate of his will on the ground that the signatures of the witnesses on a separate self-proving affidavit failed to satisfy the statutory requirements.

🏛 RULE OF LAW

Where witnesses, with the intent to attest a will, sign a self-proving affidavit but do not sign the will or an attestation clause, clear and convincing evidence of their intent should be produced to establish substantial compliance with the statutory requirements.

FACTS: Ranney signed his will in his attorney's law office, in the presence of another lawyer and a secretary. The witnesses did not sign the will itself, however. Instead, they signed a self-proving affidavit contained on a separate page. Both witnesses believed that they were signing and attesting the will, and both attorneys believed that the signatures on the affidavit complied with the statutory requirements. After Ranney's death, his wife, Betty, contested probate of Ranney's will on the ground that it failed to comply with the statutory formality requirements. The surrogate who ordered probate of the will was reversed by the law division of the superior court, but the appellate division reversed and admitted the will to probate. Betty appealed.

ISSUE: Where witnesses, with the intent to attest a will, sign a self-proving affidavit but do not sign the will or an attestation clause, should clear and convincing evidence of their intent be produced to establish substantial compliance with the statutory requirements?

HOLDING AND DECISION: (Pollock, J.) Yes. Where witnesses, with the intent to attest a will, sign a self-proving affidavit but do not sign the will or an attestation clause, clear and convincing evidence of their intent should be produced to establish substantial compliance with the statutory requirements. Substantial compliance is a functional rule designed to cure the inequity caused by the formalism of the law of wills. The primary purpose of formalities is to ensure that the document reflects the uncoerced intent of the testator. However, rigid insistence on literal compliance often frustrates this purpose. It would be ironic if such literal compliance with formalities invalidated a will that is the deliber-

ate and voluntary act of a testator. Thus, the will should be admitted to probate. Affirmed.

▶ ANALYSIS

Self-proving affidavits and attestation clauses, although substantially similar in content, serve different functions. Attestation clauses facilitate probate by providing "prima facie evidence" that the testator voluntarily signed the will in the presence of the witnesses. Self-proving affidavits, by comparison, are sworn statements by eyewitnesses that the will has been duly executed. In other words, in the attestation clause, the attestant expresses the present intent to act as a witness, while in the affidavit, the affiant swears the will has already been witnessed.

■=■

Quicknotes

ATTESTATION CLAUSE That portion of a will purporting to have testamentary effect on the testator's disposition, as attested to by witnesses.

ATTESTATION REQUIREMENTS The required actions to be taken by a witness to the execution of a document in order for that instrument to be subsequently valid.

■=■

In re Estate of Hall

Parties not identified.

Mont. Sup. Ct., 310 Mont. 486, 51 P.3d 1134 (2002).

NATURE OF CASE: Appeal from admittance of joint will to probate.

FACT SUMMARY: Hall's daughter argued that a draft of a joint will executed by Hall and his wife and notarized by their attorney in the absence of any other witnesses was invalid because it was not properly witnessed.

🏛 RULE OF LAW
It is irrelevant that a document offered for probate as a will has not been properly witnessed where clear and convincing evidence establishes the testator's intent that the document be the testator's will.

FACTS: Hall had executed a will in 1984. Then, in 1997, at the suggestion of Cannon, Hall's attorney, Hall and his wife agreed to execute a joint will. They met at Cannon's office, and ironed out the will's terms. Although the document they had worked on was a draft, Hall asked Cannon if the draft could stand as a will until Cannon sent them a final version. Cannon said that it would be valid if Hall and Hall's wife executed the draft and he notarized it, and accordingly, the couple executed the draft, and Cannon notarized it with no other witnesses present. When they returned home from the meeting, Hall apparently told his wife to tear up his 1984 will, which his wife did. After Hall's death, his wife applied to informally probate the joint will. Hall's daughter objected, arguing that the draft had been improperly witnessed (the state's law requires at least two witnesses). The lower court ordered the joint will admitted to probate, and the daughter appealed. The state's highest court granted review.

ISSUE: Is it irrelevant that a document offered for probate as a will has not been properly witnessed where clear and convincing evidence establishes the testator's intent that the document be the testator's will?

HOLDING AND DECISION: (Reginier, J.) Yes. It is irrelevant that a document offered for probate as a will has not been properly witnessed where clear and convincing evidence establishes the testator's intent that the document be the testator's will. Typically, the probate statute requires that for a will to be valid, two people must witness the testator signing the will and then sign the will themselves. However, the statute also provides that if two individuals do not properly witness the document, it may still be treated as if it had been executed under certain circumstances. One such circumstance is if the proponent of the document establishes by clear and convincing evidence that the decedent intended the document to be the decedent's will. Thus, here the issue is whether the lower court erred in concluding that Hall intended the joint will to be his will. The evidence indicates that the lower court did not err. First, the joint will specifically revoked all previous wills and codicils made by either Hall or his wife. Second, Hall directed that his prior will be destroyed. The evidence demonstrated that Hall and his wife believed that the joint will would stand as a will until Cannon provided one in cleaner, more final form. Affirmed.

▶ ANALYSIS

The doctrine under which a court may probate a document that was not properly executed if the court is satisfied that there can be no reasonable doubt that the deceased intended the document to constitute his will is known as the **dispensing power** doctrine. The dispensing power doctrine, applied in this case, is found at Uniform Probate Code § 2-503.

■■■

Quicknotes

PROBATE The administration of a decedent's estate.

TESTATOR One who executes a will.

■■■

Kimmel's Estate

Parties not identified.

Pa. Sup. Ct., 278 Pa. 435, 123 A. 405 (1924).

NATURE OF CASE: Appeal from entry of a letter into probate.

FACT SUMMARY: Kimmel, the decedent, wrote a letter to his sons mentioning, among other things, what was to happen to his possessions if anything were to happen to him. His sons attempted to probate the letter.

🏛 RULE OF LAW
An informal document evidencing intent of a conditional gift and an intent to execute may serve as a testamentary document.

FACTS: Kimmel wrote a letter to his sons which was mailed by him on the day of his death. The letter was very poorly written but contained a discussion of the weather, butchering, and a possible trip to town. It also stated, "if enny thing happens all the scock money in the 3 Bank liberty lones Post office stamps and my home on Horner St goes to George Darl and Irvin Kepp [my two sons] this letter lock it up it may help you out." The letter was dated and signed "Father." The heirs at law protested the entry of the letter into probate.

ISSUE: Can an informal document evidencing intent of a conditional gift and an intent to execute serve as a testamentary document?

HOLDING AND DECISION: (Simpson, J.) Yes. An informal document evidencing intent of a conditional gift and an intent to execute can serve as a testamentary document. In this case, Kimmel's language, however poor, telling his sons what should happen if he were not to survive clearly shows a gift that is conditional upon the occurrence of something, namely Kimmel's death. Most holographic wills are informal in character, and the fact that the weather is discussed in the document does not change its testamentary effect. Also, the fact that Kimmel signed all his letters "Father" shows that he considered this letter a final and executed document. The intent to execute is more important than Kimmel's knowledge of the formal requirements for execution. Affirmed.

▎ *ANALYSIS*

Most courts interpret conditional wills as stating the testator's inducement to execute the will rather than an actual condition that must be fulfilled before the will can be probated. For example, in *Eaton v. Brown*, 193 U.S. 411 (1904), the testator's holographic will stated: "I am going on a journey and may not return. If I do not, I leave everything to my adopted son." The testator did in fact return, only to die several months later. The court held the will entitled to probate on the grounds that her statement about not returning was merely an expression of her thoughts at the time she wrote the will, not an event that must occur in order to make the will effective.

Quicknotes

HOLOGRAPHIC WILL A will that is handwritten by the testator or testatrix.

TESTAMENTARY INTENT A determination that the document was intended to be a will and as such, reflects the writer's true wishes.

In re Estate of Kuralt

Parties not identified.

Mont. Sup. Ct., 303 Mont. 335, 15 P.3d 931 (2000).

NATURE OF CASE: Appeal from determination that a letter was a valid holographic codicil to deceased's formal will.

FACT SUMMARY: Kuralt (famous for his "On the Road" television show) wrote a letter to his mistress, Shannon, while very sick, and a couple of weeks before he died, expressing an intent that Shannon "inherit" property they had shared. Kuralt's estate argued that the letter was not a valid holographic codicil to his formal will.

🏛 RULE OF LAW
A letter written by deceased while in extremis, expressing an intent that another "inherit" a specific bequest of deceased's property and not the entirety of the deceased's estate is a valid holographic codicil to deceased's formal will.

FACTS: Charles Kuralt (Kuralt), who was a "homespun American icon" known for his television show "On the Road," had a 30-year intimate personal relationship with Shannon. Both Kuralt and Shannon desired to keep their relationship secret and were successful in doing so. In 1989, Kuralt executed a holographic will that bequeathed all of Kuralt's interest in particular real property to Shannon. Then, in 1994, Kuralt executed a formal will that did not specifically mention any of the real property owned by Kuralt. Apparently, Kuralt had intended to transfer a 90-acre parcel to Shannon in 1997, but he suddenly became very ill that year. The day he checked into a hospital, he wrote a letter to Shannon expressing his intent that she "inherit" the parcel. He sent about $17,000 with the letter. He died two weeks later, and Shannon sought to probate the letter as a valid holographic codicil to Kuralt's formal 1994 will. The estate objected, but the trial court eventually entered judgment in favor of Shannon. The state's highest court granted review.

ISSUE: Is a letter written by deceased while in extremis, expressing an intent that another "inherit" a specific bequest of deceased's property and not the entirety of the deceased's estate, a valid holographic codicil to deceased's formal will?

HOLDING AND DECISION: (Trieweiler, J.) Yes. A letter written by deceased while in extremis, expressing an intent that another "inherit" a specific bequest of deceased's property and not the entirety of the deceased's estate is a valid holographic codicil to deceased's formal will. The intent of the testator must be followed. Here, the record supports the lower court's decision. The relevant facts are that Kuralt and Shannon continued to have a family-like relationship until the day he died; that along with the letter at issue he sent Shannon significant sums of money; there was extrinsic evidence that he intended to convey the parcel to Shannon; he was in extremis (practically on his death bed); he used the word "inherit"; and the letter made a specific bequest, and did not purport to bequeath the entirety of the estate. For these reasons, the letter was a valid holographic codicil to Kuralt's formal 1994 will. Affirmed.

▌ *ANALYSIS*

The estate, and in a case that preceded this one, the dissent, argued that the letter, which said, "I'll have the lawyer visit the hospital to be sure you inherit the rest of the place…" was not a codicil but was instead an expression of a future intent to make a will. That argument focused on the precatory, versus imperative, language of the letter; the majority clearly went beyond just the letter's language in rendering its decision.

▬▬

Quicknotes

CODICIL A supplement to a will.

HOLOGRAPHIC WILL A will that is handwritten by the testator.

▬▬

Harrison v. Bird

Beneficiary (P) v. Decedent's cousin (D)

Ala. Sup. Ct., 621 So. 2d 972 (1993).

NATURE OF CASE: Appeal from a judgment of intestacy.

FACT SUMMARY: After Speer died, Harrison (P), sole beneficiary of Speer's will, filed for probate a document purporting to be Speer's last will and testament, despite the fact that Speer's attorney had torn Speer's will into four pieces after she informed him that she wanted to revoke her will.

🏛 RULE OF LAW
A rebuttable presumption of revocation exists where a will cannot be found among a deceased's personal effects.

FACTS: A year and a half after Speer executed a will naming Harrison (P) as the main beneficiary of her estate, she advised her attorney that she wanted to revoke her will. Her attorney tore the will into four pieces, informing Speer by letter that he had "revoked" her will as instructed and was sending the pieces of the will to her. State law required that, to be lawfully revoked, a will must be destroyed in the testator's presence. When Speer died, the letter was found but not the four pieces of the will. The probate court granted letters of administration to Bird (D), Speer's cousin. Harrison (P) filed for probate a duplicate of the original will. The court ruled that, although Speer's will was not lawfully revoked, there arose a presumption that Speer had revoked the will herself since the destroyed will was not found. The court held that Harrison (P) had not rebutted the presumption of revocation and that the estate should be administered as an intestate estate and confirmed the letters of administration issued to Bird (D). Harrison (P) appealed.

ISSUE: Does a rebuttable presumption of revocation exist where a will cannot be found among a deceased's personal effects?

HOLDING AND DECISION: (Houston, J.) Yes. A rebuttable presumption of revocation exists where a will cannot be found among a deceased's personal effects. Under Alabama state law, Speer's will was not lawfully revoked because her attorney destroyed it at her direction and consent but not in her presence. However, where a testator destroys the copy of the will in her possession, a presumption arises that she has revoked her will and all duplicates, even though a duplicate exists that is not in her possession. The burden of rebutting the presumption is on the proponent of the will. Under the facts of this case, there existed a presumption that Speer destroyed her will, thus revoking it. Harrison (P) did not present sufficient evidence to rebut the presumption, i.e., to convince the trier of fact that the absence of the will was not due to Speer's destroying and thus revoking the will. Affirmed.

▶ ANALYSIS

A will may be revoked either by executing a subsequent will that revokes the previous one (expressly or by inconsistency) or by physical destruction of the will, known as "performing a revocatory act on the will." Revocatory acts include tearing, burning, or obliterating the will, either completely or partially. If neither of the two steps above are taken, the will, if duly executed, will be admitted to probate.

Quicknotes

EXECUTRIX A female person designated by a deceased individual to effectuate the disposition of his property pursuant to a testamentary instrument.

INTESTATE ESTATE The property of an individual who dies without executing a valid will.

Thompson v. Royall

Parties not identified.

Va. Sup. Ct., 163 Va. 492, 175 S.E. 748 (1934).

NATURE OF CASE: Action to probate a will.

FACT SUMMARY: Kroll attempted to revoke her will and codicil by signing notations on the back of each that purported to render them void.

🏛 RULE OF LAW
Revocation of a will by cancellation is not accomplished unless the written words of the document are mutilated or otherwise impaired.

FACTS: Kroll executed an attested will that she gave to Brittain, her executor, for safekeeping. She then executed a codicil, which she signed in the presence of two attesting witnesses and gave to Coulling, the attorney who prepared both documents. She later instructed Coulling to destroy both documents but was persuaded by Coulling to retain the documents for her use in case she decided to execute a new will. She signed a statement written on the back of the will by Coulling which read, "This will null and void and to be only held by H.P. Brittain instead of being destroyed as a memorandum for another will if I desire to make same." An identical statement but substituting Coulling's name for Brittain's was written by Coulling on the back of the codicil and was signed by Kroll. Upon her death, Kroll left an estate valued at approximately $200,000. The will and codicil were offered for probate and contested by various nieces and nephews who were not mentioned in the instruments. The jury found the documents to be the last will and testament of Kroll, and from an order sustaining that verdict and probating the will, contestants brought this writ of error.

ISSUE: May a memorandum written in another's handwriting on the reverse side of a testamentary instrument and signed by the testator, purporting to void the document, effect a revocation by cancellation of the instrument?

HOLDING AND DECISION: (Hudgins, J.) No. In order to effect revocation by cancellation, the testator must actually mutilate, erase, deface, or otherwise mark the written portions of the testamentary instrument. It is true that in *Warner v. Warner's Estate*, 37 Vt. 356, one court permitted cancellation by a writing that did not actually touch written portions of the will, but that decision has not been followed and has been justly criticized by commentators. Thus, although the testatrix obviously intended to revoke her will, she did not revoke it by cancellation. Furthermore, the contestants agree that the memorandum did not constitute a "writing indicating an intention to revoke" under the appropriate statute since it was not in testatrix's own handwriting or attested to by witnesses. Therefore, the will and codicil were not revoked, and the order admitting them to probate must be affirmed.

▶ ANALYSIS

Thompson v. Royall accords with authorities generally. If words purporting to effect the cancellation of a will are written in the margin or on the reverse side of the instrument, they are ineffective to accomplish their purpose. However, the writing of words such as "void" or "canceled" will effect a revocation of a will if written across material portions of the will. The ruling of *Warner v. Warner's Estate*, disapproved by the court, is in general disrepute.

Quicknotes

CODICIL A supplement to a will.

DEVISAVIT VEL NON A matter transferred from a court of chancery to a court of law in order to determine whether a certain document was intended to be a will.

REVOCATION The cancellation or withdrawal of some authority conferred or an instrument drafted, such as the withdrawal of a revocable contract offer prior to the offeree's acceptance.

SUBSCRIBING WITNESS A person who witnesses the execution of a document and signs his name thereto.

LaCroix v. Senecal

Deceased's niece (P) v. Deceased's friend (D)

Conn. Sup. Ct., 140 Conn. 311, 99 A.2d 115 (1953).

NATURE OF CASE: Appeal from judgment holding that a residuary devise and bequest under a codicil, which was virtually identical to a similar residuary devise and bequest in deceased's will, was void, but that there was no resulting intestacy as to that portion of the residue because it was valid under the will.

FACT SUMMARY: Dupre's niece, LaCroix (P), argued that a residuary clause in Dupre's codicil, which replaced a virtually identical clause in Dupre's will, was void because it was witnessed by the spouse of a beneficiary.

🏛 RULE OF LAW
The doctrine of dependent relative revocation sustains a gift by will, when such gift has been revoked in a codicil that substantially reaffirms the gift but is void by reason of the interest of a subscribing witness.

FACTS: Dupre executed a will leaving the residue of her estate in equal shares to her nephew and her friend, Senecal (D). She then executed a codicil revoking the residuary clause of the will and replaced it with an almost identical clause. The only change was that in the will she had used her nephew's nickname and in the codicil she used both his formal name and nickname. However, Senecal's (D) husband witnessed the codicil. Under the applicable purging statute, the codicil would be valid, but the gift to Senecal (D) would be invalid. The lower court nonetheless held that the gift to Senecal (D) was valid, on the theory that the gift under the will remained valid. Dupre's niece, LaCroix (P), argued that the gift was void, and the state's supreme court granted review.

ISSUE: Does the doctrine of dependent relative revocation sustain a gift by will, when such gift has been revoked in a codicil that substantially reaffirms the gift but is void by reason of the interest of a subscribing witness?

HOLDING AND DECISION: (Brown, J.) Yes. The doctrine of dependent relative revocation sustains a gift by will, when such gift has been revoked in a codicil that substantially reaffirms the gift but is void by reason of the interest of a subscribing witness. That doctrine provides that if a testator cancels or destroys a will with a present intention of making a new one immediately and as a substitute and the new will is not made or, if made, fails of effect for any reason, it will be presumed that the testator preferred the old will to intestacy, and the old one will be admitted to probate in the absence of evidence overcoming the presumption. It is a rule of presumed intention. As to the case at hand, it would be difficult to conceive of a more deserving case for the application of the doctrine of dependent relative revocation. There is no room for doubt that the sole purpose of the testatrix in executing the codicil was, by making the very minor change in referring to her nephew, to eliminate any uncertainty as to his identity. Obviously, it was furthest from her intention to make any change in the disposition of her residuary estate. When the will and codicil are considered together, as they must be, to determine the intent of the testatrix, it is clear that her intention to revoke the will was conditioned upon the execution of a codicil which would be effective to continue the same disposition of her residuary estate. Affirmed.

▶ ANALYSIS

Most courts place limitations on the doctrine of dependent relative revocation. They require that the doctrine applies only (1) if there is an alternative plan of disposition that fails or (2) where the mistake is recited in the terms of the revoking instrument, or, is established by clear and convincing evidence.

■=■

Quicknotes

CODICIL A supplement to a will.

DEPENDENT RELATIVE REVOCATION The doctrine which states that if the same person executes a will which revokes an earlier will, the earlier will is revoked only if the latter will is effective, otherwise the earlier will remains in full effect and force.

TESTATRIX A woman who dies having drafted and executed a will or testament.

■=■

Estate of Alburn

Parties not identified.

Wis. Sup. Ct., 18 Wis. 2d 340, 118 N.W.2d 919 (1963).

NATURE OF CASE: Appeal from the admission of a will to probate.

FACT SUMMARY: Alburn revoked a will in the mistaken belief that this would reinstate an earlier revoked will.

🏛 RULE OF LAW
Where a will is mistakenly revoked in the belief that an earlier revoked will would be revived, the doctrine of dependent relative revocation may be applied to revive the mistakenly revoked will.

FACTS: Alburn, while living in Milwaukee, had a will drawn up leaving her estate to her husband's relatives. Alburn subsequently moved to Kankakee and had a new will drawn up specifically revoking the Milwaukee will. There were several changes in bequests, but the bulk of her estate was still left to the relatives of her deceased husband. Alburn then revoked the Kankakee will, based on uncontradicted testimony at the trial to probate this will, in the mistaken belief that revocation of the Kankakee will would revive the Milwaukee will. Alburn subsequently died, and her heirs alleged that she died intestate. Both the Milwaukee and Kankakee wills were offered to the probate court. The court found that the Milwaukee will had been revoked and could not be admitted. The Kankakee will was deemed to be valid under the doctrine of dependent relative revocation on the grounds that Alburn had revoked it by mistake and she had not wanted to die intestate since all of her heirs at law, one a minor, had no bequests under her wills.

ISSUE: Where a will has been revoked on the mistaken belief that this would revive an earlier revoked will, may the doctrine of dependent relative revocation be applied?

HOLDING AND DECISION: (Currie, J.) Yes. The doctrine of dependent relative revocation may also be applied to situations such as the one herein where a will is revoked in the mistaken belief that it would revive any earlier revoked will. The uncontradicted evidence establishes Alburn's mistaken belief. The testamentary scheme under the Kankakee will is closer to Alburn's testamentary plan than distribution through intestate succession would be. There is no showing that Alburn wished to die intestate or that any change in circumstances had occurred. Under this type of situation, the doctrine of dependent relative revocation should be applied. Affirmed.

▶ ANALYSIS

A few jurisdictions and the English courts hold that the revocation of a subsequently executed will revives the earlier revoked will since the revocation clause in the subsequent will has, itself, been revoked. Since a will is an ambulatory document having no legal effect until the date of the testator's death, the revocation clause is ineffective if revoked before the testator's death. *Goodright v. Glazier*, 4 Burr. 2512 (1770).

Quicknotes

DEPENDENT RELATIVE REVOCATION The doctrine which states that if the same person executes a will which revokes an earlier will, the earlier will is only revoked if the latter will is effective. Otherwise the earlier will remains in full effect and force.

ESTATE ADMINISTRATOR A person designated by a court to effectuate the disposition of a decedent's estate.

EXECUTRIX A female person designated by a deceased individual to effectuate the disposition of his property pursuant to a testamentary instrument.

LEGATEE A person who is granted a legacy or bequest pursuant to a will.

RESIDUARY CLAUSE (OF WILL) A clause contained in a will disposing of the assets remaining following distribution of the estate.

Clark v. Greenhalge

Beneficiary (P) v. Executor (D)

Mass. Sup. Ct., 411 Mass. 410, 582 N.E.2d 949 (1991).

NATURE OF CASE: Appeal from a judgment incorporating a notebook by reference into the terms of a will.

FACT SUMMARY: Although Nesmith reserved the right in her will to make a further disposition of personal property by a memorandum, Greenhalge (D), the executor, refused to comply with one of Nesmith's bequests written in a notebook.

RULE OF LAW
A properly executed will may incorporate by reference into its provisions any document or paper not so executed and witnessed if it was in existence at the time of the execution of the will and is identified by clear and satisfactory proof as the paper referred to therein.

FACTS: Nesmith executed a will, naming Greenhalge (D) as executor of her estate and also the principal beneficiary, but reserved the right to make further disposition of tangible personal property as designated by a memorandum. In addition to a memorandum list of items to be distributed, Nesmith periodically made entries into a notebook, designating bequests of personal property. One of those bequests gave Clark (P) an oil painting of a farm scene. After Nesmith's death, Greenhalge (D) complied with all her bequests, except the one for the painting. Clark (P) commenced this action to compel Greenhalge (D) to deliver the painting to her. The probate judge awarded the painting to Clark (P), and Greenhalge (D) appealed.

ISSUE: May a properly executed will incorporate by reference into its provisions any document or paper not so executed and witnessed if it was in existence at the time of the execution of the will and is identified by clear and satisfactory proof as the paper referred to therein?

HOLDING AND DECISION: (Nolan, J.) Yes. A properly executed will may incorporate by reference into its provisions any document or paper not so executed and witnessed if it was in existence at the time of the execution of the will and is identified by clear and satisfactory proof as the paper referred to therein. Here, the parties agree that the memorandum document was incorporated into the will, but Greenhalge (D) contends that the notebook was not incorporated. However, the statements in the notebook unquestionably reflect Nesmith's exercise of her right to restructure the distribution of her tangible personal property upon her death. That the

notebook is not entitled "memorandum" is of no consequence. The evidence supports the conclusion that Nesmith intended that the bequests in her notebook be accorded the same power and effect as those contained in the memorandum referenced in her will. Affirmed.

ANALYSIS

The cardinal rule in the interpretation of wills is that the intention of the testator shall prevail, provided it is consistent with the rules of law. To narrowly construe the will to exclude the notebook contents as "a memorandum" would undermine that long-standing policy. The most recent (1991) version of the Uniform Probate Code requires that a will may refer to a separate memo or list disposing of personal property, but such a list must be signed by the testator in order to be given effect.

■=■

Quicknotes

CODICIL A supplement to a will.

SPECIFIC BEQUEST A transfer of property that is accomplished by means of a testamentary instrument.

TESTATRIX A woman who dies having drafted and executed a will or testament.

■=■

Johnson v. Johnson

Parties not identified.

Okla. Sup. Ct., 279 P.2d 928 (1954).

NATURE OF CASE: Appeal from a judgment denying probate to a purported will.

FACT SUMMARY: Johnson typed a three-paragraph "will" but did not sign it or have it witnessed. Later, at the bottom of the same page, he wrote, signed, and dated a short dispositive passage.

RULE OF LAW

A valid, holographic codicil may incorporate and republish a prior will that would have been ineffective because of its failure to comply with formal requisites.

FACTS: Johnson, an experienced attorney who had drafted many valid wills for his clients, typed a three-paragraph document by which he purported to make a final disposition of his property. Although the document was apparently intended to serve as his will, he neither signed nor dated it and never had the instrument attested to. Sometime later, he added a paragraph at the bottom of the page. That paragraph, which was signed and dated, was written in Johnson's own hand. It provided in part, "To my brother James I give ten dollars only. This will shall be complete unless hereafter altered, changed or rewritten." Upon Johnson's death, the entire page, consisting of both the typed and handwritten portions, was offered for probate. The opponent of the instrument charged that the entire document constituted a single integrated will which, since it was partially typewritten, failed for want of valid execution and attestation. Its proponents claimed that the paper consisted of an invalid typewritten will and a valid holographic codicil and that the codicil republished and validated the ineffective will. The trial court denied the petition for probate, and an appellate tribunal affirmed. The proponents of the instrument then appealed to the state supreme court.

ISSUE: Can a valid, holographic codicil republish and validate a prior ineffective will?

HOLDING AND DECISION: (Per curiam) Yes. A valid, holographic codicil may incorporate and republish a prior will that would have been ineffective because of its failure to comply with formal requisites. Any writing that is properly executed may constitute a codicil if it is so intended by the testator. In this case, Johnson's handwritten paragraph qualifies as a valid codicil, and, by the weight of authority, that codicil incorporates and validates the three-paragraph will, which, but for the codicil, would have failed for want of execution and at-

testation. The judgments of the courts below must, therefore, be reversed and the will ordered admitted to probate.

CONCURRENCE: (Corn, J.) The majority's opinion is a commendable one since it implements the obvious intentions of the testator.

DISSENT: (Halley, C.J.) The language of the handwritten paragraph indicates that it was intended as an addition to the typed will and was not designed to serve as a codicil thereto. The entire page should, therefore, be deemed to constitute one will, which, because it does not comply with the statutory formalities, is ineffective and not appropriate for admission to probate.

▶ *ANALYSIS*

Most courts recognize that any will, including an invalid one, is republished and, if necessary, validated by the execution of an effective codicil. Thus, the result of the Johnson case depended on whether or not the handwritten passage added by the testator qualified as a codicil. Ordinarily, a codicil must comply with the same formal requisites as are necessary to create a valid will. Thus, a holographic codicil must be entirely handwritten, it must be signed and dated, it must be intended to serve as a testamentary instrument, and it must dispose of at least some property of the testator.

Quicknotes

CODICIL A supplement to a will.

HOLOGRAPHIC CODICIL A handwritten provision added to a testamentary instrument.

REVOCATION The cancellation or withdrawal of some authority conferred or an instrument drafted, such as the withdrawal of a revocable contract offer prior to the offeree's acceptance.

UNDUE INFLUENCE Improper influence that deprives the individual freedom of choice or substitutes another's choice for the person's own choice.

Via v. Putnam

Unidentified (D) v. Decedent's surviving spouse (P)

Fla. Sup. Ct., 626 So. 2d 460 (1995).

NATURE OF CASE: Appeal from summary judgment in a probate action.

FACT SUMMARY: Rachel Putnam (P), the surviving spouse, sought recovery from a forced share but the decedent's children claimed that mutual wills executed by their parents prior to the marriage of their father to Putnam (P) gave them priority status.

🏛 RULE OF LAW
Children, as third-party beneficiaries under mutual wills of parents, should not be given creditor status when their interests contravene the interests of a surviving spouse under the pretermitted spouse statute.

FACTS: Edgar and Joann Putnam executed mutual wills in 1985 that left their estate to their children after the death of both. After Joann died, Edgar married Rachel (P) but did not prepare a new will. Following Edgar's death, Rachel (P) filed a claim for a statutory share. Edgar's children filed (D) competing claims based on the mutual wills executed by their parents. The trial judge granted summary judgment to the children, holding that they were third-party beneficiaries under the wills and entitled to priority creditor status to the entire estate above Rachel's (P) interest as a pretermitted spouse. Rachel (P) appealed and the district court reversed.

ISSUE: Should children, as third-party beneficiaries under mutual wills of parents, be given creditor status when their interest contravene the interests of a surviving spouse under the pretermitted spouse statute?

HOLDING AND DECISION: (Overton, J.) No. Children, as third-party beneficiaries under mutual wills of parents, should not be given creditor status when their interest contravene the interests of a surviving spouse under the pretermitted spouse statute. The pretermitted spouse statute allows the surviving spouse to take a share as if the decedent died intestate where the will was made before marriage. The legislature, with its strong public policy in protecting surviving spouses, did not intend for third-party beneficiaries of previously executed mutual wills to take priority. While it is true that other jurisdictions have taken the opposite position for a variety of reasons, public policy reasons argue strongly for giving priority to the surviving spouse. Additionally, the legislature expressly provided exceptions to the pretermitted spouse statute. To hold that third-party beneficiaries of previously executed wills could take priority would essentially amend these statutory exceptions. Accordingly, the district court is affirmed and Rachel Putnam (P) is entitled to her statutory share of the estate.

▶ *ANALYSIS*

This is the minority view on this issue. The majority view, where third party beneficiaries have priority, has interesting implications for the status of property while the testator is still alive. Jurisdictions have differed on where property subsequently acquired fits within this scheme.

Quicknotes

CREDITOR A person or party to whom a debt or obligation is owed.

PRETERMITTED Omitted; usually refers to an heir who is unintentionally omitted from a testator's will.

THIRD-PARTY BENEFICIARY A party who benefits from a promise made pursuant to a contract although he is not a party to the agreement.

CHAPTER 5

Nonprobate Transfers and Planning for Incapacity

Quick Reference Rules of Law

Farkas v. Williams

Estate administrators (P) v. Beneficiary (D)

III. Sup. Ct., 5 III. 2d 417, 125 N.E.2d 600 (1955).

NATURE OF CASE: Action to determine who, between the administrators of the estate and the beneficiary of the trust, had a right to four stock certificates.

FACT SUMMARY: The administrators (P) of Farkas's estate claim the right to four stock certificates that Farkas held in trust for Williams (D).

RULE OF LAW
Even though the settlor retains the power to revoke the trust and appoints himself as trustee, if the beneficiary obtains any interest in the trust before the settlor dies, a valid inter vivos trust may have been formed.

FACTS: Albert Farkas executed a written declaration of trust for four separate stock certificates and named Williams (D) as beneficiary of all four. Farkas retained the power to revoke the trust and the power to vote, sell, redeem, exchange, or otherwise deal with the stock. He also appointed himself as trustee. If Farkas didn't revoke the trust, Williams (D) was required to be alive when Farkas died or the trust would be automatically revoked. Farkas died without having revoked the trust, and the administrators (P) of his estate brought this action to obtain a declaration of rights to the stock certificates. The administrators (P) claimed that the trust was testamentary and not valid because Farkas had not complied with the Statute of Wills in making his declarations of trust. They claimed that Farkas had retained so much control over the trust that it didn't qualify as an inter vivos trust. The circuit court held that the trust was an invalid testamentary trust, and so the stock was an asset of the Farkas estate.

ISSUE: Must a beneficiary obtain some interest in the trust before the settlor dies to have a valid inter vivos trust?

HOLDING AND DECISION: (Hershey, J.) Yes. It is necessary that a beneficiary obtain some interest in the trust prior to the time the settlor dies or the trust will be considered to be a testamentary trust. This means that the settlor cannot retain absolute control over the trust res in making an inter vivos trust. It is true that Farkas retained a great deal of control over the trust res, but Williams (D) did have an interest in the trust before Farkas died. Farkas had to administer the trust in accordance with the declaration of trust, which limited his control over the stock. Even though Williams (D) was required to be living when Farkas died in order to have any right to the stock, which meant that he did not have an interest that he could bequeath to anyone, he still had a small right

to the stock in that, if the trust were not revoked and Farkas, as trustee, committed a breach of trust, Williams (D) could hold the estate liable. A valid inter vivos trust was established in Williams's (D) favor. Reversed.

ANALYSIS

There is a split of opinion among the different jurisdictions as to the amount of power and control the settlor can retain and still have a valid inter vivos trust. The more recent cases seem to hold as the court in this case did. They allow the settlor to retain a great deal of control over the trust.

Quicknotes

INTER VIVOS TRUST Property that is held by one person for the benefit of another and which is created by an instrument that takes effect during the life of the grantor.

REVOCABLE TRUST The holding of property by one party for the benefit of another pursuant to an instrument in which the creator reserves the right to revoke the trust.

TESTAMENTARY DISPOSITION A disposition of property that is effective upon the death of the grantor.

Wilhoit v. Peoples Life Insurance Co.

Beneficiary (P) v. Insurance company (D)

218 F.2d 887 (7th Cir. 1955).

NATURE OF CASE: Action to recover money held in trust.

FACT SUMMARY: Sarah Wilhoit arranged for Peoples Life Insurance Company (D) to hold the proceeds of her husband's life insurance policy in trust. She then bequeathed the trust corpus to the son (P) of her stepson.

🏛 RULE OF LAW
A party who establishes a trust consisting of the proceeds of a life insurance policy may, by will, designate a trust beneficiary other than the one named in the trust instrument.

FACTS: As designated beneficiary, Sarah Wilhoit was entitled to receive the proceeds of her husband's Peoples Life Insurance Company (D) policy. She rejected an option that would have involved leaving the proceeds with Peoples (D) in exchange for interest payments at the minimum rate of 3 percent per annum. Instead, she elected to have Peoples (D) pay the proceeds, amounting to nearly $5,000, directly to her. Twenty-three days after acknowledging receipt of the money, she returned it to the company with instructions to hold it in trust, subject to withdrawal upon demand, at a minimum annual interest rate of 3½ percent. The trust arrangement, which was expressly accepted by Peoples (D), provided for distribution of the corpus to Robert G. Owens, Sarah's brother, in the event of her death. Robert G. Owens died in 1932; Sarah Wilhoit lived until 1951, then died, leaving a will in which she bequeathed the money in the trust to Robert Wilhoit (P), son of her stepson. At Sarah's death, the estate of Robert G. Owens was reopened, and his son, Thomas (D), legatee under his father's will, joined a newly appointed administrator (D) of the estate of Robert G. Owens in seeking the trust corpus for Thomas (D). Peoples (D) paid the money into court, leaving Robert Wilhoit (P) and Thomas Owens (D) to litigate the issue of who should receive the money. Owens (D) argued that the trust instrument constituted an insurance contract and that the parties' rights should be determined by insurance law rather than the provisions of the statute of wills. Accordingly, Owens (D) contended, Sarah Wilhoit had had no right to remove Robert G. Owens as beneficiary of the trust. Robert Wilhoit (P) disputed these contentions, claiming that the trust arrangement constituted nothing more than a contract of deposit, that the provision in favor of Robert G. Owens was invalid as an attempted testamentary disposition, and that any interest created in favor of Robert G. Owens had

been extinguished upon his death before Sarah Wilhoit died. The trial court granted Robert Wilhoit's (P) motion for summary judgment and awarded the trust corpus to Wilhoit (P). Thomas Owens (D), together with the administrator (D) of his father's estate, then appealed.

ISSUE: May a party who has established a trust consisting of the proceeds of her spouse's life insurance policy include a provision in her will that has the effect of changing the beneficiary designated in the trust agreement?

HOLDING AND DECISION: (Major, J.) Yes. A party who establishes a trust consisting of the proceeds of a life insurance policy may, by will, designate a trust beneficiary other than the one named in the trust instrument. The agreement between Sarah Wilhoit and the company (D) appears to have been a separate and independent contract and was neither an insurance contract nor supplemental thereto in the sense that Thomas Owens (P) has argued. Sarah Wilhoit had the option of leaving the policy proceeds on deposit with Peoples (D) but instead entered into a different arrangement of her own creation. By the terms of this arrangement, she designated Robert G. Owens to receive the trust corpus in the event of her death. She obviously did not intend his estate to receive the money if he predeceased her because, after his death, she bequeathed the money to someone else. Therefore, the trial court committed no error in awarding the trust corpus to Robert Wilhoit (P).

▶ ANALYSIS

The contract entered into by Mrs. Wilhoit is an illustration of a valid type of will substitute. She created an interest in her own favor but included a provision by which her interest would have passed to Robert G. Owens had he not predeceased her. Will substitutes which incorporate or direct the distribution of an insurance policy or its proceeds are usually recognized as valid, although similar instruments which do not involve insurance policies or proceeds may be unenforceable by reason of their failure to comply with the appropriate wills statute. In this connection, note that the court observes that the Indiana wills statute would have invalidated Sarah Wilhoit's contract had it been entered into with a bank rather than an insurance company.

■■■■

Continued on next page.

Quicknotes

SUCCESSOR BENEFICIARY A beneficiary who succeeds to the interest of an earlier beneficiary whose interest in the property has terminated.

TRUST The holding of property by one party for the benefit of another.

Estate of Hillowitz

Executors (P) v. Widow (D)

N.Y. Ct. App., 22 N.Y.2d 107, 238 N.E.2d 723 (1968).

NATURE OF CASE: Action to recover the interest of a decedent in a partnership.

FACT SUMMARY: Pursuant to a partnership agreement, Hillowitz's share of an investment club passed to his widow (D). His executors (P) claimed that this asset should have passed to his estate.

🏛 RULE OF LAW
A partnership agreement clause providing that each partner's interest, upon his death, shall pass to his spouse, is valid and enforceable.

FACTS: Hillowitz was a partner in an investment club. A clause in the club's partnership agreement recited that, in the event of the death of any partner, his interest would pass to his wife, without any termination of the partnership arrangement. When Hillowitz died, the club, in compliance with the terms of the partnership agreement, paid to his widow (D) the sum of $2,800, which amount represented Hillowitz's share of the partnership. The executors (P) of Hillowitz's estate then brought an action against Mrs. Hillowitz (D). The executors (D) contended that the provision of the partnership agreement was invalid because it constituted an attempted testamentary disposition but did not comply with the requisites of the statute of wills. Hillowitz's interest in the partnership, the executors (P) argued, should therefore have been included as an asset of his estate. Mrs. Hillowitz (D), by way of defense, maintained that the provision of the partnership agreement constituted a valid and enforceable contract. The trial court sustained Mrs. Hillowitz's (D) argument, but the appellate division reversed. Mrs. Hillowitz (D) appealed.

ISSUE: Is a partnership agreement provision which recites that each partner's interest, upon his death, shall pass to his spouse, invalid as an attempted testamentary disposition?

HOLDING AND DECISION: (Fuld, C.J.) No. A partnership agreement clause providing that each partner's interest, upon his death, shall pass to his spouse, is valid and enforceable. Such a provision is indistinguishable in form from an ordinary third-party beneficiary contract. Like the typical provision that recites that the interest of a deceased partner shall pass to the surviving members of the partnership, the clause involved in this case is not testamentary in nature and need not comply with the formalities of the statute of wills. Therefore, Mrs. Hillowitz (D) is entitled to retain the $2,800 that was received from her husband's investment club. Reversed.

▶ ANALYSIS

Many interests which vest only after the death of the party who controls their disposition are nevertheless deemed not to be testamentary in nature. Examples of interests of this type include the benefits of an insurance policy and the proceeds of an employee pension plan. In many states, legislative enactments exempt certain interests from the status of testamentary dispositions. This enables these interests to vest without the necessity of complying with the formal requisites of a jurisdiction's wills statute.

■■■

Quicknotes

INTER VIVOS TRUST Property that is held by one person for the benefit of another and which is created by an instrument that takes effect during the life of the grantor.

LIFE ESTATE An interest in land measured by the life of the tenant or a third party.

THIRD-PARTY BENEFICIARY A party who benefits from a promise made pursuant to a contract although he is not a party to the agreement.

■■■

Egelhoff v. Egelhoff

Decedent's child (P) v. Decedent's ex-wife (D)

532 U.S. 141 (2001).

NATURE OF THE CASE: Appeal from decision distributing proceeds of insurance policy and pension plan.

FACT SUMMARY: Donna Rae Egelhoff (D) received the proceeds from an insurance plan and a pension plan provided by her ex-husband's employer after he died intestate from injuries incurred in a traffic accident. The decedent had not removed her name as beneficiary. The decedent's two children from a previous marriage, David and Samantha Egelhoff (P), his statutory heirs, sued Donna Egelhoff (D) for the proceeds from the plans.

🏛 RULE OF LAW

ERISA preempts a state statute that provides for the automatic revocation of a spouse as the designated beneficiary of a nonprobate asset upon the couple's divorce.

FACTS: David A. Egelhoff had named his wife, Donna Rae Egelhoff (D), beneficiary of an insurance policy and a pension plan provided through his employer, Boeing Company. Both plans were governed by the Employee Retirement Income Security Act of 1974 (ERISA). Two months after the couple's divorce, David died intestate after a traffic accident. He had not removed Donna's (D) name as beneficiary under either plan. Donna (D) received $46,000 from the life insurance policy. David and Samantha Egelhoff (P), the decedent's children from a previous marriage and his statutory heirs, sued Donna (D) for the life insurance proceeds, relying on a Washington statute that provided that the designation of a spouse as beneficiary of a nonprobate asset would be revoked automatically upon the couple's divorce. David and Samantha (P) also filed a separate action to recover the pension plan proceeds. [The trial courts granted summary judgment for Donna (D), holding that both the insurance policy and the pension should follow ERISA's procedures. The appellate court consolidated the cases and concluded that ERISA did not preempt the state statute and that David and Samantha (P) were not entitled to the proceeds. The state supreme court affirmed. The U.S. Supreme Court granted review.]

ISSUE: Does ERISA preempt a state statute that provides for the automatic revocation of a spouse as the designated beneficiary of a nonprobate asset upon the couple's divorce?

HOLDING AND DECISION: (Thomas, J.) Yes. ERISA preempts a state statute that provides for the auto-

matic revocation of a spouse as the designated beneficiary of a nonprobate asset upon the couple's divorce. Under ERISA's preemption section, 29 U.S.C. section 1144(a), ERISA supersedes all state laws that relate to employee benefit plans that are covered by ERISA. The provision must be given broad effect. A state law "relates to" an ERISA plan if there is a "connection with" the plan. Here, the Washington statute impermissibly restricts ERISA plan administrators' choice of rules in determining whom to designate as beneficiary. Hence, it has a connection with ERISA plans. Further, the statute interferes with ERISA's ability to administer a plan uniformly throughout the country. An ERISA administrator should not be burdened with the task of trying to find out if a purported beneficiary has in fact had her beneficiary's status revoked. Reversed.

DISSENT: (Breyer, J.) Merely because a state's law imposes some burden on the administration of an ERISA plan does not by itself mandate preemption. The statute at issue here is no different from many such state laws. It imposes at most an administrative burden, but in substance it promotes ERISA objectives—it transfers an employee's pension assets at death to those individuals whom the worker would likely have wanted to receive them. The assumption under the state statute here—that a divorced worker would prefer that a child rather than a divorced spouse receive those assets—is embodied in the Uniform Probate Code and is consistent with human experience. The effect of the majority's holding that statute preempted is that the ex-wife will receive a windfall at the expense of the deceased's children. Applying the majority's rationale would also preempt other transfer statutes, such as those involving simultaneous deaths or spousal murder.

▶ ANALYSIS

Although it is not federal common law, divorce sets aside a revocable beneficiary designation of a former spouse under both the Restatement 3d of Property and the UPC.

▪━▪

Quicknotes

POWER OF REVOCATION The power to revoke an existing interest.

▪━▪

Bush v. Schiavo

State's governor (P) v. Persistent-vegetative-state incompetent's guardian (D)

Fla. Sup. Ct., 885 So. 2d 321 (2004).

NATURE OF CASE: Appeal from affirmance of judgment that a statute permitting a state's governor to stay removal of artificial life-prolonging measures of a person in a persistent vegetative state is an unconstitutional violation of separation of powers.

FACT SUMMARY: The state legislature passed legislation enabling the governor to stay removal of artificial life-prolonging measures of a person in a persistent vegetative state, despite a court's determination that the person would have elected to terminate the life-prolonging procedures. Schiavo (P), husband to Theresa (Terri) Schiavo, who had been in a persistent vegetative state for 10 years, argued that the legislation was an unconstitutional violation of separation of powers.

RULE OF LAW

A statute authorizing a state's governor to stay removal of artificial life-prolonging measures of a person in a persistent vegetative state, despite a court's determination that the person would have elected to terminate the life-prolonging procedures, is an unconstitutional violation of separation of powers.

FACTS: Theresa (Terri) Schiavo was in a persistent vegetative state for many years. Her husband, Schiavo (P), serving as her guardian, at the eighth year, petitioned the guardianship court to authorize the termination of life-prolonging procedures. The guardianship court issued an extensive written order authorizing the discontinuance of artificial life support. The trial court found by clear and convincing evidence that Terri was in a persistent vegetative state and that she would elect to cease life-prolonging procedures if she were competent to make her own decision. This order was affirmed on direct appeal, and Terri's nutrition and hydration tube was removed. Six days later, the state legislature passed legislation authorizing the state's governor to stay the removal of nutrition and hydration on facts that matched those applicable to Terri's situation. The state's governor then immediately issued an executive order to stay the removal of the nutrition and hydration. Schiavo (P) successfully challenged the constitutionally of the legislation in the lower courts, and the state's court granted review.

ISSUE: Is a statute authorizing a state's governor to stay removal of artificial life-prolonging measures of a person in a persistent vegetative state, despite a court's determination

that the person would have elected to terminate the life-prolonging procedures, an unconstitutional violation of separation of powers?

HOLDING AND DECISION: (Pariente, C.J.) Yes. A statute authorizing a state's governor to stay removal of artificial life-prolonging measures of a person in a persistent vegetative state, despite a court's determination that the person would have elected to terminate the life-prolonging procedures, is an unconstitutional violation of separation of powers. Under the express separation of powers provision in the state constitution, the judiciary is a coequal branch of the state government vested with the sole authority to exercise the judicial power, and the legislature cannot, short of constitutional amendment, reallocate the balance of power expressly delineated in the constitution among the three coequal branches. The statute at issue, as applied in this case, resulted in an executive order that effectively reversed a properly rendered final judgment and thereby constituted an unconstitutional encroachment on the power that has been reserved for the independent judiciary. When the prescribed procedures are followed according to our rules of court and the governing statutes, a final judgment is issued, and all post-judgment procedures are followed, it is without question an invasion of the authority of the judicial branch for the legislature to pass a law that allows the executive branch to interfere with the final judicial determination in a case. That is precisely what occurred here and for that reason the statute is unconstitutional as applied to Theresa Schiavo. In addition, the statute is unconstitutional on its face because it delegates legislative power to the executive by giving the governor uncircumscribed, unfettered discretion over stays of life-prolonging procedures because it does not specify adequate standards for the application of the legislative authority delegated thereunder.

▶ *ANALYSIS*

Florida's Governor Bush petitioned the U.S. Supreme Court for certiorari in this case but the petition was denied in January 2005. That, however, was not the end of legislative attempts to keep Terri Schiavo alive; Congress, in a special session devoted exclusively to the Schiavo case, and seemingly in contravention of separation of powers, passed legislation with President Bush's approval, for federal court

Continued on next page.

review of the case; the federal courts, however, sustained removal of nutrition and hydration. Terri Schiavo died on March 31, 2005, two weeks after her life-sustaining tube was removed. Having been in a persistent vegetative state, she was most likely oblivious to the fact that she had become the center of a national right-to-die battle that had constitutional ramifications.

■≡■

Quicknotes

SEPARATION OF POWERS The system of checks and balances preventing one branch of government from infringing upon exercising the powers of another branch of government.

■≡■

CHAPTER 6

Construction of Wills

Quick Reference Rules of Law

Mahoney v. Grainger

Parties not identified.

Mass. Sup. Ct., 283 Mass. 189, 186 N.E. 86 (1933).

NATURE OF CASE: Appeal from a decree denying a petition for distribution of a legacy under a will.

FACT SUMMARY: After a trial judge found that a testatrix's sole heir at law was her maternal aunt, ruling that statements of the testatrix were admissible only insofar as they gave evidence of the material circumstances surrounding the testatrix at the time of the execution of the will, her first cousins appealed the ruling, contending they were her heirs at law.

🏛 RULE OF LAW
A will duly executed and allowed by the court must, under the statute of wills, be accepted as the final expression of the intent of the person executing it.

FACTS: Sullivan told her attorney she wanted to make a will. She left the bulk of her estate to two first cousins and told the attorney that the rest of the estate should be shared equally by "about twenty-five first cousins." The attorney subsequently drafted the will containing a residuary clause stating in part: "All the rest and residue of my estate, both real and personal property, I give, devise and bequeath to my heirs at law living at the time of my decease." After Sullivan's death, the trial judge found that Sullivan's sole heir at law at the time of her death was her maternal aunt, Frances Greene. The first cousins argued that Sullivan's statement regarding the twenty-five first cousins should be admitted to prove her testamentary intention. However, the trial judge ruled that the statements were not admissible to prove intention and dismissed the cousins' petition. They appealed.

ISSUE: Must a will duly executed and allowed by the court, under the statute of wills, be accepted as the final expression of the intent of the person executing it?

HOLDING AND DECISION: (Rugg, C.J.) Yes. A will duly executed and allowed by the court must, under the statute of wills, be accepted as the final expression of the intent of the person executing it. It is only where testamentary language is not clear in its application to facts that evidence may be introduced in order to clarify the language. In this case, there is no doubt as to Sullivan's heirs at law. The aunt alone falls within that description. The cousins are excluded. The circumstance that the plural word "heirs" was used does not prevent one individual from taking the entire gift. Decree affirmed.

▶ ANALYSIS

Most courts subscribe to the rule that when an instrument has been proved and allowed as a will, oral testimony as to the meaning and purpose of a testator cannot be used to disturb the plain meaning of a will. The fact that a will does not conform to the instructions given to the draftsman who prepared it, by reason of mistake or otherwise, does not authorize a court to reform or alter the will or remold it by amendments. Where no doubt exists as to the property bequeathed or the identity of the beneficiary, there is no room for extrinsic evidence.

Quicknotes

EXTRINSIC EVIDENCE Evidence that is not contained within the text of a document or contract but which is derived from the parties' statements or the circumstances under which the agreement was made.

RESIDUARY CLAUSE (OF WILL) A clause contained in a will disposing of the assets remaining following distribution of the estate.

TESTATRIX A woman who dies having drafted and executed a will or testament.

Arnheiter v. Arnheiter

Parties not identified.

N.J. Super. Ch. Div., 42 N.J. Super. 71, 125 A.2d 914 (1956).

NATURE OF CASE: Application to correct mistake in probated will.

FACT SUMMARY: Executrix (P) of Guterl's will applied to the court to correct an obvious mistake in the will by changing the street number of property devised to correctly identify property owned by Guterl.

RULE OF LAW
An erroneous description of a particular devise will not cause the devise to fail, where less essential particulars can be eliminated leaving a resulting description that is clearly accurate.

FACTS: Upon Guterl's death, her will was duly probated. The will provided that the executrix (P) was to sell Guterl's half interest in the property known as "304" Harrison Avenue, and to use the proceeds to establish trusts for her nieces. At the time of the execution of her will and at her death, Guterl owned a half interest in "317" Harrison Avenue, not "304" Harrison Avenue. This was the only property on Harrison Avenue in which Guterl held any interest. The executrix (P) applied to the court to correct the will, changing "304" to "317."

ISSUE: Will an erroneous description of a particular devise cause a devise to fail, where less essential particulars can be eliminated, leaving a resulting description that is clearly accurate?

HOLDING AND DECISION: (Sullivan, J.) No. An erroneous description of a particular devise will not cause the devise to fail, where less essential particulars can be eliminated leaving a resulting description that is clearly accurate. The court is powerless to reform the will in the manner requested by the executrix (P), reformation is not available to change a testamentary instrument. But where there is an obvious mistake, the court may delete particulars from the description of a particular devise so long as the resulting description fits. Here, the mistake was clear, Guterl owned no interest in "304" Harrison Avenue. By disregarding the street number, the rest of the description is sufficient to identify the property described, as her interest in "317" Harrison Avenue, and the will should be so construed. Judgment entered.

▶ ANALYSIS

This is the doctrine of "falsa demonstratio non nocet," which allows courts to prevent devises from failing. The key in applying the doctrine is that after the "false" or less important particular is dropped from the description, whether the object or subject of the devise can be identified with sufficient certainty. If not, the devise will still fail.

■═■

Quicknotes

EXECUTRIX A female person designated by a deceased individual to effectuate the disposition of his property pursuant to a testamentary instrument.

■═■

Erickson v. Erickson

Decedent's child (P) v. Decedent's widow (D)

Conn. Sup. Ct., 716 A.2d. 92 (1998).

NATURE OF CASE: Appeal from judgment in a probate action.

FACT SUMMARY: Ronald Erickson executed a will two days before getting married that was intended to leave his estate to his future wife but technically did not provide for the contingency of a subsequent marriage.

RULE OF LAW
Extrinsic evidence is admissible to establish the intent of a testator that his will is valid notwithstanding a subsequent marriage if a scrivener's error led the testator to believe that it would be valid.

FACTS: Ronald Erickson, the father of three children (P), executed a will in 1988 that left his estate to his future wife, Dorothy (D), or if she predeceased him, then to his children. Two days later, he married Dorothy (D). Eight years later, Ronald died and his will was admitted to probate. His children (P) claimed that the will was invalid because it did not provide for the contingency of marriage. The probate court refused to admit extrinsic evidence of Ronald's intent but held that the circumstances surrounding the execution of the will demonstrated that it provided for the contingency of marriage, and the judgment was appealed.

ISSUE: Is extrinsic evidence admissible to establish the intent of a testator that his will is valid notwithstanding a subsequent marriage?

HOLDING AND DECISION: (Borden, J.) Yes. Extrinsic evidence is admissible to establish the intent of a testator that his will is valid notwithstanding a subsequent marriage if a scrivener's error led the testator to believe that it would be valid. The question of whether a will provides for the contingency of a subsequent marriage must be determined without resort to extrinsic evidence. Thus, the will should not have been admitted by the trial court on that basis. However, that does not end the matter because this Court is prepared to reverse a prior decision on the admissibility of extrinsic evidence. The dissenting view in that case argued that there are three principal reasons for admitting extrinsic evidence of a scrivener's mistake. First, there is no discernible policy difference for distinguishing between innocent mistakes and fraud or duress and undue influence when it comes to extrinsic evidence. Second, the risk of subverting the intent of the testator is no greater than the risk of enforcing an instrument that misstates the intent.

Third, although signing a will creates a strong presumption it represents the testator's intentions, that presumption is rebuttable; and the narrowness of the exception would not likely give rise to a proliferation of groundless will contests. Accordingly, the rule is now that extrinsic evidence of a scrivener's mistake is admissible to show the testator's intent. Therefore, while Erickson's will is not valid on the basis that it provided for the contingency of a subsequent marriage, extrinsic evidence may be introduced to prove that he intended it to be valid after the marriage but that this intent was frustrated by a mistake. Reversed and remanded.

ANALYSIS

The prior case that was overruled was *Connecticut Junior Republic v. Sharon Hospital*, 448 A.d. 190 (1982). It was decided by a 3-2 vote and event the majority acknowledged that the time may come when it should be reversed. The court noted that it did not believe that any testators were relying on the previous rule by deliberately omitting language providing for the contingency of marriage in order to be sure that it would be revoked later.

Quicknotes

SCRIVENER Writer of legal documents.

TESTATOR One who executes a will.

Estate of Russell

Parties not identified.

Cal. Sup. Ct., 69 Cal. 2d 200, 444 P.2d 353 (1968).

NATURE OF CASE: Appeal from a determination of heirship.

FACT SUMMARY: The testator left her $10 gold piece and diamonds to Hembree, her only heir-at-law, and the residue of her estate to Charles Quinn and Roxy Russell, the latter being her dog, who predeceased her.

🏛️ **RULE OF LAW**
When an uncertainty arises upon the face of a will, it cannot always be determined whether the will is ambiguous or not until the circumstances surrounding the writing of the will are first considered.

FACTS: The testatrix left her $10 gold piece to her sister, Hembree, who was her only heir-at-law, and the residue of her estate to Charles Quinn and Roxy Russell. Charles was a longtime friend and confidante, while Roxy was testatrix's dog. Roxy predeceased the testatrix but was alive at the time of execution of the will. Extrinsic evidence was introduced to establish Roxy's identity. The trial court found that it was the testatrix's intention that Charles was to receive the entire residue and that the gift to Roxy was merely precatory in nature. It further found that there was no lapse of the gift to Charles but that the gift was to maintain Roxy. Hembree appealed, arguing that the gift of one-half of the residue to a dog was clear and unambiguous; that it was void and passed to her under the laws of intestate succession; and that the admission of extrinsic evidence did not cure the invalidity of the gift.

ISSUE: When an uncertainty arises upon the face of a will, can it always be determined whether the will is ambiguous or not until the circumstances surrounding its writing are first considered?

HOLDING AND DECISION: (Sullivan, J.) No. When an uncertainty arises upon the face of a will, it cannot always be determined whether the will is ambiguous or not until the circumstances surrounding the writing of the will are first considered. The exclusion of extrinsic evidence regarding surrounding circumstances merely because no ambiguity appears can easily lead to giving the will a meaning never intended. California Probate Code § 105 provides that if, after the admission of extrinsic evidence, the will is not susceptible to two or more meanings, then no ambiguity exists. The statute simply delineates the manner of ascertaining testator's intention. Here, the trial court's conclusion was unreasonable. No words gave the residuary all to Charles or appeared to be merely precatory in nature. A distribution in equal shares to two persons cannot be said to be for one to use whatever portion is necessary in behalf of the other. No extrinsic evidence should have been admitted that would lead to a meaning to which the will was not reasonably susceptible. As for the gift to Roxy, it was clearly void so it lapsed and passed to the heirs-at-law by intestacy. Hembree, as the only heir-at-law, should take the gift. Reversed.

▶ *ANALYSIS*

Few definite guidelines can be given as to interpretation of wills. Rules and "trends" are conflicting. The rules of the case above apply not only to wills but to contracts and deeds also. They are important in evidence cases as well. What evidence to admit is usually the tough question. The student can only consider the appropriate statutory provisions and the various theories presented in the cases and resolve the problem in his own mind.

▬▬■

Quicknotes

EXTRINSIC EVIDENCE Evidence that is not contained within the text of a document or contract but which is derived from the parties' statements or the circumstances under which the agreement was made.

RESIDUE That property which remains following the distribution of the assets of the testator's estate.

TESTATRIX A woman who dies having drafted and executed a will or testament.

▬▬■

Allen v. Talley

Decendent's nephew (P) v. Decedent's sister (D)

Tex. App. II Dist., 949 S.W.2d 59 (1997).

NATURE OF CASE: Appeal from summary judgment in a probate action.

FACT SUMMARY: Mary Shoults executed a will that left her estate to her living brothers and sisters, but the children of her deceased siblings claimed they were entitled to a share.

RULE OF LAW
The words "living brother and sisters" in the general provision of a will should be construed as words of survivorship.

FACTS: Mary Shoults executed a will in which she left her property to her "living brothers and sisters . . . to share and share alike" at a time when she had three brothers and two sisters. When she died, only her sister Lera Talley (D) and brother Claude Allen were alive. Lewis Allen (P), the son of Shoults's deceased brother, filed a petition claiming that the words of the will were not words of survivorship, did not create a class gift, and that the anti-lapse statute applied. If this position were correct, Allen (P) and the other children of the deceased siblings would be entitled to a share of Shoults's estate. The trial court disagreed and ruled that Talley (D) and Claude Allen were the only ones to inherit under the will.

ISSUE: Should the words "living brothers and sisters" in the general provision of a will be construed as words of survivorship?

HOLDING AND DECISION: (Wright, J.) Yes. The words "living brothers and sisters" in the general provision of a will should be construed as words of survivorship. The primary concern of the court in the construction of a will is to determine the testator's intent. The intent must be ascertained by reviewing the will in its entirety. In the absence of ambiguity, the will must be construed on the basis of the express language used and the common and ordinary meaning of the terms used. In the instant case, Shoults's will contained one general provision devising her estate to her "living brothers and sisters." It is clear and plain from this statement that she intended only her living siblings to participate in the ownership of her estate. Thus, they are words of survivorship and the antilapse statute is inapplicable. Talley (D) and Claude Allen should share the estate equally. Affirmed.

ANALYSIS

An antilapse statute applies only where there is no contrary intention in the will. The majority rule is that an express survivorship requirement defeats use of the antilapse statute. In 1990, the Uniform Probate Code was revised to hold that words of survivorship do not necessarily defeat use of the antilapse statute.

Quicknotes

SURVIVORSHIP Between two or more persons, such as in a joint tenancy relationship, the right to the property of a deceased passes to the survivor.

Dawson v. Yucus

Beneficiary (P) v. Executrix (D)

Ill. App. Ct., 97 Ill. App. 2d 101, 239 N.E.2d 305 (1968).

NATURE OF CASE: Appeal from a judgment for defendants in an action to construe a will.

FACT SUMMARY: Wilson (P), the remaining beneficiary of a will, argued that the gift was made to a class and therefore, as survivor of the class, he was entitled to the entire interest bequeathed to the class.

🏛️ **RULE OF LAW**
Where the number of beneficiaries to a gift is certain, and the share each is to receive is also certain and in no way dependent for its amount upon the number who shall survive, it is not a gift to a class but to the individuals.

FACTS: Nelle Stewart left a duly executed will containing ten clauses. The second clause gave the one-fifth interest in farm lands that Stewart inherited from her husband to two of his nephews, Stewart Wilson and Gene Burtle. Each was to receive one-half of Stewart's one-fifth interest. After the will was admitted to probate, Wilson (P) filed suit against the executrix, Yucus (D), to construe the will, alleging that the devise was a class gift, that Burtle had died after the date of execution of the will but before the testatrix, and that Wilson (P), as the survivor of the class, was entitled to the entire one-fifth interest in the farm. Burtle's two children, Dawson (P) and Burtle (P), were subsequently substituted as plaintiffs. The trial court held that clause two did not create a class gift, and therefore the gift to Burtle lapsed and passed into the residue of the estate upon his death. Dawson (P) and Burtle (P) appealed.

ISSUE: Where the number of beneficiaries to a gift is certain, and the share each is to receive is also certain and in no way dependent for its amount upon the number who shall survive, is it a gift to a class?

HOLDING AND DECISION: (Jones, J.) No. Where the number of beneficiaries to a gift is certain, and the share each is to receive is also certain and in no way dependent for its amount upon the number who shall survive, it is not a gift to a class but to the individuals. In this case, Stewart named the individuals, giving them each a specified portion of her interest in the farm, thus making certain the number of beneficiaries and the share each was to receive. The shares in no way depend upon the number who shall survive Stewart's death. She did, however, create a survivorship gift of the residue of her estate, thus indicating she knew how to manifest such an intent. Hence, the language of clause two, phrased differently, was intended to create a gift to individuals distributively. Affirmed.

▶ **ANALYSIS**

A testator is deemed to be "group minded," that is, intends to create a class gift, if she uses a generic class label such as "to my nephews" in devising her property. Stewart stated in her bequest in clause two that she believed the farm lands should go back to her late husband's "side of the house." Wilson argued unsuccessfully that this phrase, together with the extrinsic evidence admitted by the court as to Stewart's intentions, clearly required class gift construction.

Quicknotes

CLASS GIFT A gift to a group of unspecified persons whose number, identity, and share of the gift will be determined sometime in the future.

EXTRINSIC EVIDENCE Evidence that is not contained within the text of a document or contract but which is derived from the parties' statements or the circumstances under which the agreement was made.

REMAINDER An interest in land that remains after the termination of the immediately preceding estate.

RESIDUE That property which remains following the distribution of the assets of the testator's estate.

Wasserman v. Cohen

Trust beneficiary (P) v. Trustee (D)

Mass. Sup. Jud. Ct., 414 Mass. 172, 606 N.E.2d 901 (1993).

NATURE OF CASE: Appeal from dismissal of an action for declaratory judgment against the surviving trustee of a revocable inter vivos trust.

FACT SUMMARY: Wasserman (P) sought the proceeds from the sale of a building that would have been conveyed to her through a revocable inter vivos trust at the settlor's death had the settlor not sold the building prior to her death.

🏛 RULE OF LAW

When a testator disposes, during his lifetime, of the subject of a specific gift of real estate contained in a revocable inter vivos trust, that gift is held to be adeemed by extinction.

FACTS: Drapkin created a memorial trust, naming herself both settlor and trustee. She funded the trust with "certain property" delivered on the date of execution, retaining the right to add property by inter vivos transfer and by will. Drapkin also reserved the right to amend or revoke the trust and to withdraw property from the trust. When she executed the trust, Drapkin held record title to an apartment building. However, Drapkin sold the property before she died and never conveyed her interest in the property to the trust. Wasserman (P) brought an action for declaratory judgment, requesting that Cohen (D) be ordered to pay to Wasserman (P) the proceeds from the sale of the building. The probate judge dismissed the action. Wasserman (P) appealed.

ISSUE: When a testator disposes, during his lifetime, of the subject of a specific gift of real estate contained in a revocable inter vivos trust, is that gift held to be adeemed by extinction?

HOLDING AND DECISION: (Lynch, J.) Yes. When a testator disposes, during his lifetime, of the subject of a specific gift of real estate contained in a revocable inter vivos trust, that gift is held to be adeemed by extinction. To be effective, a specific legacy or devise must be in existence and owned by the testator at the time of her death. A trust is construed according to the same rules traditionally applied to wills. Here, Drapkin created the trust along with her will as part of a comprehensive estate plan. There is no reason to apply a different rule because she conveyed the property under the terms of the trust rather than her will. Thus, the doctrine of ademption applies to the trust, and the devise of the apartment building was adeemed by Drapkin. Affirmed.

▶ ANALYSIS

Wasserman (P) had argued that deciding ademption questions based on a determination that a devise is general or specific is overly formalistic and fails to serve the testator's likely intent. However, the court found that, at least in regard to the conveyance of real estate, determining whether a devise is general or specific is the proper first step in deciding questions of ademption. The court noted that the so-called harsh results of the doctrine can easily be avoided by careful draftsmanship, and its existence must be recognized by any competent practitioner.

Quicknotes

ADEMPTION Revocation of a specific devise or bequest made pursuant to a testamentary instrument if the particular property is not part of the decedent's estate at the time of death.

INTER VIVOS TRUST Property that is held by one person for the benefit of another and which is created by an instrument that takes effect during the life of the grantor.

RESIDUARY ESTATE That portion of the estate which remains after all the estate has been distributed through the satisfaction of all claims and is conditional upon something remaining after the claims on the testator's estate are satisfied.

SETTLOR The grantor or donor of property that is to be held in trust for the benefit of another.

Restrictions on the Power of Disposition: Protection of the Spouse and Children

Quick Reference Rules of Law

In re Estate of Cross

Parties not identified.

Ohio Sup. Ct., 664 N.E.2d 905 (1996).

NATURE OF CASE: Appeal from probate court decision.

FACT SUMMARY: In probate, the court ruled that Cross's surviving spouse was entitled to take an intestate share against the will although her support needs were being taken care of by Medicaid.

🏛 RULE OF LAW
An election by a surviving spouse to take against a will may be required because the nonutilization of available income renders Medicaid recipients ineligible.

FACTS: Carroll Cross died with a will leaving his entire estate to his son, Ray. At the time of the death, Beulah Cross, the surviving spouse, was very ill and living in a nursing home supported by Medicaid. A commissioner appointed by the probate court determined that Beulah should elect to take a statutory intestate share against the will, and the probate court approved. While Ray Cross appealed the decision, Beulah died, and the court of appeals reversed, holding that the election by Beulah was not necessary for her adequate support.

ISSUE: May an election by a surviving spouse to take against a will be required because the nonutilization of available income renders Medicaid recipients ineligible?

HOLDING AND DECISION: (Sweeney, J.) Yes. An election by a surviving spouse to take against a will may be required because the nonutilization of available income renders Medicaid recipients ineligible. Probate courts may elect for surviving spouses to take against the will if it finds that the election is necessary to provide adequate support for the surviving spouse taking into consideration available resources, present and anticipated needs. Eligibility for Medicaid benefits is dependent upon a recipient's income and available resources. These resources include those in which the recipient has a legal interest or ability to use. An intestate share as a surviving spouse is clearly a legal interest that qualifies as an available resource for purposes of Medicaid qualifications. Accordingly, Medicaid rules specifically hold that the nonutilization of income or resources renders a recipient ineligible. Thus, in the instant case, if Beulah Cross did not avail herself of her interest as a surviving spouse, she would have been ruled ineligible for Medicaid. The election to take against the will was necessary for her future support. The court of appeals is reversed and the judgment of the probate court is reinstated.

▶ ANALYSIS

This decision is in accord with rulings in Wisconsin and New York. However, some would argue that it is somewhat inconsistent with the rule that creditors cannot force a surviving spouse to take an elective share. Some states apply a strict mathematical formula when determining whether taking against the will is in the best interests of the surviving spouse rather the consideration of all the factors as was seen in this case.

■=■

In re Estate of Cooper

Same-sex lover of deceased (P) v. Court (D)

N.Y. App. Div. 2d Dept., Div., 187 A.D.2d 128, 592 N.Y.S.2d 797 (1993).

NATURE OF CASE: Appeal from a decree denying the right of a spouse's election to the surviving member of a same-sex relationship.

FACT SUMMARY: After Cooper's death, Chin (P), his current same-sex lover, petitioned the court to elect to take a statutory share of Cooper's estate as a "surviving spouse" rather than take his share under the will.

RULE OF LAW
The survivor of a homosexual relationship alleged to be a "spousal relationship" is not entitled to exercise a right of election against the decedent's will.

FACTS: Cooper died testate, leaving a portion of his estate to his current homosexual lover, Chin (P), and the other portion to his former homosexual lover. Chin (P), submitting evidence of a "spousal relationship," petitioned the court for the statutory right of election against Cooper's will. Chin (P) alleged that the only reason he and Cooper were not married was that the state unconstitutionally made it impossible for two people of the same sex to obtain a marriage license. He argued further that interpreting the term "surviving spouse" to exclude homosexual life partners violated the equal protection clause of the state constitution. The court held that persons of the same sex have no constitutional rights to enter into a marriage with each other, and the survivor of such a relationship had no right to elect against a decedent's will. Chin (P) appealed.

ISSUE: Is the survivor of a homosexual relationship entitled to exercise a right of election against the decedent's will?

HOLDING AND DECISION: (Mangano, J.) No. The survivor of a homosexual relationship is not entitled to exercise a right of election against the decedent's will. Where a testator disposes of his entire estate by will and is survived by a spouse, the surviving spouse may elect to take a one-third share of the net estate if the decedent is survived by one or more issue. In all other cases, the spouse is entitled to one-half of such net estate. However, the term "surviving spouse" does not include homosexual life partners. Here, any equal protection analysis must be measured by the rational basis standard. That standard has been applied in other similar instances in refuting challenges to classifications based on sexual orientation. Purported homosexual marriages do not give rise to any statutory rights, and no constitutional rights have been abrogated or violated by so holding. Accordingly, the decree is affirmed.

▶ ANALYSIS

In a 1993 Hawaii case, three same-sex couples brought suit, claiming that the Hawaii law that denied marriage licenses to same-sex couples was a denial of equal protection. Unlike the Cooper court, the Hawaii Supreme Court applied a strict scrutiny standard and held that the state must have a "compelling" interest in forbidding such marriages. *Baehr v. Lewin*, 852 P.2d 44 (Haw. 1993). The case was remanded to give the state an opportunity to substantiate its compelling interest.

Quicknotes

ELECTIVE SHARE   Election by the surviving spouse to take either what the deceased spouse gave under the will or a share of the deceased spouse's estate as set forth by statute.

EQUAL PROTECTION   A constitutional guarantee that no person shall be denied the same protection of the laws enjoyed by other persons in life circumstances.

RATIONAL BASIS REVIEW   A test employed by the court to determine the validity of a statute in equal protection actions, whereby the court determines whether the challenged statute is rationally related to the achievement of a legitimate state interest.

Sullivan v. Burkin

Widow (P) v. Successor trustee (D)

Mass. Sup. Jud. Ct., 390 Mass. 864, 460 N.E.2d 571 (1984).

NATURE OF CASE: Appeal from a dismissal of a complaint for determination of estate assets.

FACT SUMMARY: Sullivan (P) contended that the value of real estate placed in trust by her late husband should be considered part of his estate for purposes of providing her a portion of the estate.

RULE OF LAW
The surviving spouse has no claim against the assets of a valid inter vivos trust created by the deceased spouse even when the deceased spouse retained substantial rights and powers under the trust instrument.

FACTS: Sullivan's (P) husband, the decedent, executed during his life a deed of trust by which he transferred real estate to a trust with himself as sole trustee. The net income of the trust was payable to him during his life, and the trustee was instructed to pay to him all or such part of the principal that he might request. Upon his death, the trust indicated that the trustee was to pay the principal amount and any undistributed income to third parties. Sullivan executed a will wherein he stated that he intentionally neglected to make any provision for his wife, Sullivan (P). Following her husband's death, Sullivan (P) made a claim against the estate, contending that the property in the trust should be considered part of the estate. Burkin (D) was the successor in interest to the third parties to whom the decedent left the residue of the trust. The probate court held that a valid inter vivos trust was created and that the property of the trust was not to be considered part of the estate. Sullivan (P) appealed.

ISSUE: May a surviving spouse claim against the assets of a valid inter vivos trust created by the deceased spouse even when the deceased spouse retained substantial rights and powers under the trust instrument?

HOLDING AND DECISION: (Wilkins, J.) No. The surviving spouse may not claim against the assets of a valid inter vivos trust created by the deceased spouse even when the deceased spouse retained substantial rights and powers under the trust instrument. Merely because the inter vivos trust was testamentary does not indicate that it was invalid. Merely because the settlor retained a broad power to modify or revoke the trust, the law of the state is quite clear in upholding inter vivos trusts which become testamentary in nature. Further, Sullivan (P) has no special interest that should be recognized

in breaking the trust. As a result, because this trust was created under the then-established law, the assets of the trust cannot be applied to the estate. Affirmed.

▶ ANALYSIS

The court indicated quite clearly that although it felt obligated to apply the general rule in this case, it announced that in the future any inter vivos trust created or amended after the date of this opinion shall no longer follow the previously announced rule. In the future, if the settlor retains the same type of substantial rights that the decendent did in the principal case, then the assets of the trust will be considered part of the estate for purposes of distribution to the heirs of the estate.

━━■

Quicknotes

INTER VIVOS TRUST Property that is held by one person for the benefit of another and which is created by an instrument that takes effect during the life of the grantor.

REMAINDER INTEREST An interest in land that remains after the termination of the immediately preceding estate.

SUCCESSOR TRUSTEE A trustee who succeeds a previous trustee.

━━■

In re Estate of Garbade

Parties not identified.

N.Y. App. Div., 221 A.D.2d 844 (1995).

NATURE OF CASE: Appeal from decision to set aside notice of surviving spouse's election.

FACT SUMMARY: Decedent's wife claimed that the prenuptial agreement she signed should be invalidated because of the surrounding circumstances.

🏛 RULE OF LAW
A duly executed prenuptial agreement is given the same presumption of validity as any other contract in the absence of fraud.

FACTS: The Garbades were married on February 2, 1990. Decedent was a wealthy business owner who asked his future wife to sign a prenuptial agreement that waived her right to any of his property or an elective share of his estate. The agreement was prepared by decedent's attorney and, although she was advised to obtain independent counsel, decedent's wife signed the agreement without even reading it. Additionally, she did not receive a copy of the agreement. When Mr. Garbade died two years later, his wife filed a notice of election to take the surviving spouse's share. Garbade's two sons, the heirs to the estate, argued that the prenuptial agreement waived her right to take an elective share. The court agreed and set aside the notice of election. Decedent's wife appealed.

ISSUE: Is a duly executed prenuptial agreement given the same presumption of validity as any other contract in the absence of fraud?

HOLDING AND DECISION: (Mercure, J.) Yes. A duly executed prenuptial agreement is given the same presumption of validity as any other contract in the absence of fraud. The party attacking the validity of an agreement has the burden of coming forward with evidence of fraud, which will not be presumed. In the instant case, decedent's wife presented evidence that she did not raise the issue of a prenuptial agreement, that it was not prepared until very shortly before the wedding, that it was not executed until hours before, and that she was not aware of its provisions. Even assuming that all of these allegations are correct, they do not demonstrate evidence of fraud. She has established nothing more than her own dereliction in failing to learn more about a legal agreement she signed. Accordingly, the prenuptial agreement is valid and the decedent's wife is not entitled to an elective share. Affirmed.

▶ ANALYSIS

Some courts have found that prenuptial agreements are invalid due to the undue influence of one spouse over the other. These courts have held that prenuptial agreements should be scrutinized more than other agreements. The basis for this additional scrutiny is that the relationship between future spouses is different in many respects than other relationships between contracting parties.

■≡■

Quicknotes

PRENUPTIAL AGREEMENT An agreement entered into by two individuals in contemplation of marriage, determining their rights and interests in property upon dissolution or death

■≡■

Estate of Shannon

Surviving spouse (P) v. Court (D)

Cal. Ct. App., 224 Cal. App. 3d 1148 (1990).

NATURE OF CASE: Appeal from an order denying a petition for a determination of heirship as an omitted spouse.

FACT SUMMARY: When Russell Shannon died, after marrying Lila (P) and without changing the will he had executed twelve years before the marriage, Lila (P) argued that she should be entitled to estate distribution as an omitted surviving spouse.

RULE OF LAW

If a testator fails to provide by will for a surviving spouse who married the testator after the execution of the will, the omitted spouse shall receive a statutorily prescribed share of the estate.

FACTS: Twelve years after executing his last will and testament, Russell Shannon, a widower, married Lila (P). Russell died less than two years later, without making any changes in his will, which named his daughter Beatrice as executrix and sole beneficiary. Lila (P) filed a petition for determination of entitlement to estate distribution as an omitted surviving spouse, which the probate court denied. Lila (P) appealed. When Lila (P) died while the appeal was pending, her son was named executor of her estate and substituted in her place as appellant.

ISSUE: If a testator fails to provide by will for a surviving spouse who married the testator after the execution of the will, shall the omitted spouse receive a statutorily prescribed share of the estate?

HOLDING AND DECISION: (Huffman, J.) Yes. If a testator fails to provide by will for a surviving spouse who married the testator after the execution of the will, the omitted spouse shall receive a statutorily prescribed share of the estate. The rule reflects a strong statutory presumption of revocation of the will as to the omitted spouse based upon public policy. Because Russell failed to provide for Lila (P) in his will, she is an omitted spouse. The will on its face does not manifest any intent by Russell to disinherit Lila (P). Furthermore, a general disinheritance clause in a will is insufficient to avoid the statutory presumption. Finally, no provision was made for Lila (P) outside the will nor did she make a valid agreement waiving her right to share in Russell's estate. Thus, Beatrice has not rebutted the presumption of revocation. Reversed and remanded.

ANALYSIS

The rule applied here is found in § 6560 of the California Probate Code, which essentially tracks the 1990 Uniform Probate Code. Under the statute, an omitted spouse receives a share of the estate as if the deceased had died intestate. The exceptions to that rule are listed in § 6561 and occur where the will clearly shows that the omission was intentional, the testator provided for the spouse by transfer outside the will in lieu of a testamentary provision, or the spouse made a valid waiver of the right to share in the testator's estate.

Quicknotes

DISINHERITANCE CLAUSE A clause in a testamentary instrument expressly denying a person, who would ordinarily be an heir of the testator, from the right to take a portion of the estate.

SURVIVING SPOUSE The spouse who remains living after the death of the other spouse.

Lambeff v. Farmers Co-operative Executors & Trustees Ltd.

Decedent's daughter (P) v. Estate's executors (D)

So. Australia Sup. Ct., 56 S.A.S.R. 323, 1991 WL 1121294 (1991).

NATURE OF CASE: Claim for maintenance against decedent's estate under Australia's Inheritance (Family Provision) Act.

FACT SUMMARY: Lambeff (P), decedent's daughter, who was abandoned by decedent when she was ten, claimed that she was entitled to support (provision) in the form of a legacy out of decedent's estate under Australia's Inheritance (Family Provision) Act because decedent had failed to support her "advancement in life."

🏛 RULE OF LAW
Under Australia's Inheritance (Family Provision) Act, an independent adult child of a decedent, who was abandoned by the decedent as a child, has a claim of support (provision) against decedent's estate where the child has done nothing disentitling and would have done better with proper support for the child's proper advancement in life.

FACTS: Lambeff (P) was abandoned by decedent when she was ten. Decedent left Lambeff (P) and her mother, and started another family, in which he had two sons. Lambeff (P) was not married, had a steady job, and had considerable equity in a flat. Decedent's will left his entire estate to his two sons, after payment of all debts and funeral expenses. Both sons had families to support and few assets. Lambeff (P) claimed that she was entitled to support (provision) under Australia's Inheritance (Family Provision) Act, which provides in pertinent part that a decedent's family member who is left without adequate provision for proper advancement in life may make a claim for support against the decedent's estate, which may be granted at the court's discretion.

ISSUE: Under Australia's Inheritance (Family Provision) Act, does an independent adult child of a decedent, who was abandoned by the decedent as a child, have a claim of support (provision) against decedent's estate where the child has done nothing disentitling and would have done better with proper support for the child's proper advancement in life?

HOLDING AND DECISION: (Matheson, J.) Yes. Under Australia's Inheritance (Family Provision) Act, an independent adult child of a decedent, who was abandoned by the decedent as a child, has a claim of support (provision) against decedent's estate where the child has done nothing disentitling and would have done better with proper support for the child's proper advancement in life. The statute's words "ad-

vancement in life" have a wide meaning and are not restricted to early childhood. In every case, the court must place itself in the testator's position and consider what he or she should have done as a "wise and just" testator. Here, although it is true that Lambeff (P) has done reasonably well in life without her father's support, she would have done better with proper support for her advancement in life. Given all the circumstances of the case—that she is independent and that the sons need to support families and do not have many assets—the legacy to Lambeff (P) should be modest. It is ordered that she be paid $20,000 out of the estate.

▶ ANALYSIS

The model under which this case was decided is known as the family maintenance model, which gives courts the power to determine the morality of both the decedent's dispositive scheme and survivors' claims. Proponents argue that this performs a vital social welfare function. Critics assert that such judicial discretion is a "terrible price" to pay for improved support of dependents in that it would introduce complexity and unpredictability, undermine estate planning, and hamper the orderly transfer of property rights.

■▬■

Quicknotes

DECENDENT A person who is deceased.

■▬■

Azcunce v. Estate of Azcunce

After-born child of deceased (P) v. Estate (D)

Fla. 3d Dist. App., 586 So. 2d 1216 (1991).

NATURE OF CASE: Appeal from an order denying a petition to obtain a statutory share.

FACT SUMMARY: When Azcunce died shortly after executing a second codicil to his will, which republished the original will, Patricia (P), who had been born prior to the execution of the second codicil, petitioned the court for a share of her father's estate as a pretermitted child.

RULE OF LAW

When a testator fails to provide in his will for any of his children born after making the will, the child shall receive a share of the estate equal in value to that he would have received if the testator had died intestate, unless it appears the omission was intentional.

FACTS: Azcunce executed a will, establishing a trust for his surviving spouse and his then-born children. The will contained no provision for after-born children. Azcunce subsequently executed two codicils, which republished all the terms of the original will, without altering the testamentary disposition or making provision for after-born children. Between the execution of the two codicils, Azcunce's fourth child, Patricia (P), was born. Azcunce died shortly after executing the second codicil. After the will and the two codicils were admitted to probate, Patricia (P) filed this petition, seeking a statutory share of her father's estate as a pretermitted child. The trial court denied the petition. This appeal followed.

ISSUE: When a testator fails to provide in his will for any of his children born after making the will, shall the child receive a share of the estate equal in value to that he would have received if the testator had died intestate, unless it appears the omission was intentional?

HOLDING AND DECISION: (Hubbart, J.) Yes. When a testator fails to provide in his will for any of his children born after making the will, the child shall receive a share of the estate equal in value to that he would have received if the testator had died intestate, unless it appears the omission was intentional. Without dispute, Patricia (P) was a pretermitted child both at the time her father's will was executed and at the first time the first codicil was executed. However, when the second codicil republished the original will and first codicil, Patricia's (P) prior status as a pretermitted child was destroyed, inasmuch as she was alive at the time. Presumably, if her father had wished to provide for Patricia (P), he would have done so in the second codicil. Because he did not, Patricia (P) was, in effect, disinherited. Affirmed.

ANALYSIS

The rule of § 732.302, Florida Statutes (1985) was applied here by the court of appeals. Such pretermitted heir statutes are intended to protect children from being unintentionally disinherited. Patricia (P) had argued that the will and the two codicils were somehow ambiguous and that the court should have accepted parol evidence that her father intended to provide for her. The court found utterly no ambiguity that would authorize the taking of parol evidence.

Quicknotes

CODICIL A supplement to a will.

PRETERMITTED Omitted; usually refers to an heir who is unintentionally omitted from a testator's will.

STATUTORY SHARE The statutory scheme pursuant to which property is distributed in the absence of a valid will.

In re Estate of Laura

Parties not identified.

N.H. Sup. Ct., 690 A.2d 1011 (1997).

NATURE OF CASE: Appeal from probate court decision.

FACT SUMMARY: Laura executed a will that intentionally omitted and disinherited his son and grandchildren, and the grandchildren's issue claimed they were entitled to a share of the estate.

🏛 **RULE OF LAW**
Testators who specifically name an heir in an effort to disinherit have "referred to" the issue of that heir for that purpose as well.

FACTS: Edward Laura Sr. executed a will in 1984 that provided his estate would pass to his daughter Shirley. In one paragraph, he intentionally omitted and disinherited Edward Jr. and his grandchildren Richard and Neil. The will did not mention two great-grandchildren, one of whom was born a day before the will was executed and one born two years later. In 1990, Laura attempted to execute a codicil which altered the disposition, but it was not properly witnessed. Thus, the 1984 will was presented to probate when Laura died in 1990. The great-grandchildren challenged the will on the ground that they were entitled to an intestate share as pretermitted heirs under the statutory scheme. The probate master, approved by the court, held that the great-grandchildren did not qualify as pretermitted heirs, and they appealed.

ISSUE: Have testators who specifically name an heir in an effort to disinherit "referred to" the issue of that heir for that purpose as well?

HOLDING AND DECISION: (Thayer, J.) Yes. Testators who specifically name an heir in an effort to disinherit have "referred to" the issue of that heir for that purpose as well. The applicable New Hampshire law provides that the omission of a child or issue of a child from a will is accidental unless there is evidence that the omission was intentional. This law is an attempt to effectuate the testator's presumed intent. In the instant case, the great-grandchildren argue that they are entitled to an intestate share because they were not named in the will. However, where the testator intentionally omits the parent of an otherwise pretermitted heir, that is sufficient to show that the issue of that parent was also intended to be omitted. This is supported by other decisions in which we have held that a reference to an heir need not be direct to be exculsionary. Accordingly, since the father of the great-grandchildren was expressly and intentionally disinherited by the 1984 will, the great-grandchildren were also effectively disinherited and are not entitled to an intestate share. Affirmed.

▶ **ANALYSIS**

Problems can arise when reasons for a disinheritance are provided in a will. It is possible that statements made can be libelous. In one New York case, an ex-husband sued the decedent's estate for remarks made in her will and ended up taking nearly half the estate.

■—■

Quicknotes

DISINHERITANCE CLAUSE A clause in a testamentary instrument expressly denying a person, who would ordinarily be an heir of the testator, from the right to take a portion of the estate.

TESTATOR One who executes a will.

■—■

Trusts: Creation, Types, and Characteristics

Quick Reference Rules of Law

Jimenez v. Lee

Trustee's daughter (P) v. Trustee (D)

Or. Sup. Ct., 274 Or. 457, 547 P.2d 126 (1976).

NATURE OF CASE: Action for an accounting.

FACT SUMMARY: Jimenez (P) sought an accounting from her father, Lee (D), for his use of trust funds to satisfy his legal support obligations to her.

> ## 🏛 RULE OF LAW
> Where funds are held in trust for a specific purpose, the trustee will be liable for all expenditures not related to that purpose.

FACTS: Jimenez's (P) grandmother purchased a $1,000 savings bond shortly after Jimenez's (P) birth in the joint names of Jimenez (P) and/or her father, Lee (D). The bond was for Jimenez's (P) educational needs. Another $500 bond was purchased by a third party for Jimenez's (P) education. Lee (D) subsequently cashed the bonds in and invested the proceeds in common stock, which Lee (D) held as custodian for Jimenez (P) under the Uniform Gift to Minors Act. Lee (D) had held these funds as trustee and could only use them for a proper trust purpose, Jimenez's (P) education. Jimenez (P) sought an accounting. Lee (D) alleged that no trust existed and that all funds had been used for Jimenez's (P) benefit. The trial court dismissed Jimenez's (P) complaint.

ISSUE: May a trustee use trust funds for the benefit of the beneficiary but for purposes not authorized under the trust?

HOLDING AND DECISION: (O'Connell, C.J.) No. A trustee may only use trust funds in a manner authorized under the trust. He may not expand his powers to include unauthorized uses. The evidence indicates that the bonds were to be used for Jimenez's (P) education and were held in trust by Lee (D) for this purpose. The evidence clearly establishes that Lee (D) could not expand his powers by using the bonds to purchase stock, with Lee (D) acting as custodian under the Uniform Gift to Minors Act. The stock is directly traceable to the bonds, and the trust is impressed on the stock. As trustee, Lee (D) was obligated to keep exact records of all expenditures made for Jimenez's (P) education. Failure to keep accurate records can result in a surcharge to the trustee for unaccounted sums. The trustee is also liable for expenditures not related to the purpose of the trust. Reversed and remanded.

▶ ANALYSIS

Jimenez is important for a number of reasons. First, it points up the importance of keeping adequate records of expenditures. Even if the trustee has acted entirely properly, he will be liable for any unaccounted-for funds. *White v. Rankin*, 46 N.Y.S. 228 (1897). Next, *Jimenez* indicates that the trustee must be able to establish that all expenditures are within the areas permitted under the trust instrument. Bogart on Trusts and Trustees § 972(1) (1962).

〓

Quicknotes

TRUSTEE A person who is entrusted to keep or administer property for the benefit of another.

〓

The Hebrew University Association v. Nye

Parties not identified.

Conn. Sup. Ct., 169 A.2d 641 (1961).

NATURE OF CASE: Appeal from judgment in action over property ownership.

FACT SUMMARY: Yahuda owned an extensive library that she promised to give to a university in Jerusalem but never delivered before her death.

🏛 RULE OF LAW
An imperfect gift due to lack of delivery may not be turned into a trust without an express manifestation of intent.

FACTS: Yahuda became the owner of a collection of rare manuscripts on the death of her husband. In January 1953, Yahuda went to Israel and had discussions about the library with the university officers and announced her gift of the manuscripts to them at a luncheon. Thereafter, Yahuda told everyone that she had given the library of books to the university, and she refused offers to sell. In 1954, Yahuda began arranging and cataloguing the materials for shipment to Israel. However, before her tasks were finished and the books delivered, Yahuda died. Her will left her estate to another charitable institution. The university filed suit claiming that it was entitled to the library because it was the rightful owner. The trial court ruled for the university on the basis that Yahuda had created a trust with regard to the library in favor of the university. The decision was appealed.

ISSUE: May an imperfect gift due to lack of delivery be turned into a trust without an express manifestation of intent?

HOLDING AND DECISION: (King, J.) No. An imperfect gift due to lack of delivery may not be turned into a trust without an express manifestation of intent. If an intended gift fails because there was not actual or constructive delivery, the intent can be carried out in equity under the fiction that the donor presumed to constitute himself as trustee to make the delivery. However, this is not true unless there is an express trust, which may be oral, created by the donor. In the present case, there are no facts suggesting that Yahuda ever intended to impose on herself the duties of a trustee with regard to the library. The only evidence is that she had a donative intent but failed to make the delivery. There simply is no evidence to support the trial court's conclusion that she established a trust in favor of the university. Reversed and remanded for a new trial so that the university can present another theory of ownership.

▶ ANALYSIS

Other jurisdictions may have reached a different conclusion on these facts. The Connecticut opinion here represents a strict and narrow view of what is required to show that a donor considers him or herself to be a trustee. While the court seemed to realize that Yahuda had clearly intended the university (P) to receive the library, they seemed concerned that it was subverting the rules on gifts and trusts to fit it in.

■■■

Quicknotes

DONOR A person who gives real or personal property or value.

TRUSTEE A person who is entrusted to keep or administer property for the benefit of another.

■■■

The Hebrew University Association v. Nye

Parties not identified.

Conn. Sup. Ct., 223 A.2d 397 (1966).

NATURE OF CASE: Action to resolve ownership of decedent's property.

FACT SUMMARY: The ownership of Yahuda's rare book collection was disputed because she intended to give it as a gift but died before delivering it.

🏛 RULE OF LAW
Constructive delivery of a gift through an informal document is permitted if accompanied by acts and declarations showing an intention to complete the gift.

FACTS: Yahuda became the owner of a collection of rare manuscripts on the death of her husband. In January 1953, Yahuda went to Israel and had discussion about the library with the university officers and announced her gift of it to them at a luncheon. Thereafter, Yahuda told everyone that she had given the library of books to the university, and she refused offers to sell. In 1954, Yahuda began arranging and cataloguing the materials for shipment to Israel. However, before her tasks were finished and the books delivered, Yahuda died. Her will left her estate to another charitable institution. The university filed suit claiming that it was entitled to the library because it was the rightful owner. The trial court ruled for the university on the basis that Yahuda had created a trust with regard to the library in favor of the university. After the Supreme Court reversed, the case was remanded so that the university could present alternative theories.

ISSUE: Is constructive delivery of a gift through an informal document permitted if accompanied by acts and declarations showing an intention to complete the gift?

HOLDING AND DECISION: (Parskey, J.) Yes. Constructive delivery of a gift through an informal document is permitted if accompanied by acts and declarations showing an intention to complete the gift. Constructive delivery must be the reasonable equivalent of actual delivery depending on the nature of the property and the circumstances. In the present case, Yahuda clearly indicated her intent to give the library of rare books to the university. She was preparing it for actual delivery when she died, and she had already given the university a memorandum containing a list of the contents of the library. If this memorandum was a formal document the gift would have been unquestionably valid. But the lack of formalism is not fatal here, especially given the other facts that show a clear intention to provide the gift to the university. While the court realizes that the facts here stretch the concept of constructive delivery, courts of equity must do their best to effectuate the wishes of the decedent. Thus, the university is entitled to the possession of Yahuda's library.

▶ ANALYSIS

The result reached here seems to be the most fair one possible. However, even the court was a bit apprehensive at stretching the rules to make sure that Yahuda's intent was carried out. They acknowledged that loose rules could give rise to fraudulent claims.

■══■

Quicknotes

CONSTRUCTIVE DELIVERY The transfer of title or possession of property by means other than actual delivery indicative of the parties' intent to effect a transfer.

■══■

Unthank v. Rippstein

Promisee (P) v. Executor (D)

Tex. Sup. Ct., 386 S.W.2d 134 (1964).

NATURE OF CASE: Action to declare a trust.

FACT SUMMARY: Craft sent a letter to Rippstein (P) promising to give her $200 per month.

🏛 RULE OF LAW
A mere promise to give periodic gifts in the future will not support a finding that a trust has been established.

FACTS: Craft sent Rippstein (P) a letter a few days before his death promising to give her $200 per month. The letter stated that Craft's estate would be liable for such payments if he died. Rippstein (P) alleged that the letter created an enforceable trust. Unthank (D), the executor of Craft's will, alleged that this was an unenforceable gift or a voluntary trust that was unenforceable for lack of consideration.

ISSUE: Is a mere promise to make payments in the future enforceable as a trust?

HOLDING AND DECISION: (Steakley, J.) No. A gift or voluntary trust is merely a promise, without consideration to make payments in the future. As such, it is unenforceable under the rules governing gifts. It is not a trust since there is no res and no intention expressed to hold all of the alleged trustor's property liable for payment. Upon the death of the promisor, the promise cannot be enforced against the estate since the gift of payments after death is a will substitute lacking the requisite testamentary requirements. The gift is unenforceable.

▶ ANALYSIS

Before a trust may be found to be enforceable, the equitable title must sufficiently rest in the beneficiary so as to allow him to maintain an action for the conversion of the trust property. *Flick v. Baldwin*, 141 Tex. 340. Where there is no specific trust res to which the trust is to attach, the beneficiary has no beneficial interest in any particular property. Additionally, of course, the absence of a trust res would, in and of itself, cause the trust to fail in most instances.

Quicknotes

HOLOGRAPHIC CODICIL A handwritten provision added to a testamentary instrument.

TRUST The holding of property by one party for the benefit of another.

TRUST CORPUS The aggregate body of assets placed into a trust.

VOLUNTARY TRUST A trust established by a settlor voluntarily, as opposed to by operation of law, with the intent to make a gift of the trust property for the benefit of another.

Speelman v. Pascal

Promisee (P) v. Widow of producer (D)

N.Y. Ct. App., 10 N.Y.2d 313, 178 N.E.2d 723, 222 N.Y.S.2d 324 (1961).

NATURE OF CASE: Action to enforce a gift of future profits.

FACT SUMMARY: Prior to his death, Pascal's (D) husband sent Speelman (P) a letter in which he promised to give Speelman (P) a share of the profits from his future production of a musical.

> ## 🏛 RULE OF LAW
> A gift of property to be acquired in the future is valid and effective if the donor manifests an irrevocable intention to make a present transfer of his interest.

FACTS: Pascal, a theatrical producer, owned an exclusive license to create stage and film versions of a musical based on George Bernard Shaw's "Pygmalion." About two years before this license was due to expire, Pascal sent a letter to Speelman (P) (also known as Kingman) in which he promised her shares of his profits from the anticipated productions. Although Pascal died several months later, arrangements were later made, through his estate, for the production of the well-known and highly successful musical "My Fair Lady." Speelman (P) then sought to enforce Pascal's promise to give her a share of the production's profits, but Pascal's widow (D) claimed that the gift was not enforceable since it had referred to profits not yet in existence. The trial court rendered judgment in favor of Speelman (P), but Mrs. Pascal (D) appealed.

ISSUE: May a valid gift be created of property not yet in existence?

HOLDING AND DECISION: (Desmond, C.J.) Yes. A gift of property to be acquired in the future is valid and effective if the donor manifests an irrevocable intention to make a present transfer of his interest. This rule enjoys general acceptance in this jurisdiction. In this case, delivery of Pascal's letter constituted an adequate expression of his intention to make a present gift of future profits from his anticipated production. Accordingly, the gift to Speelman (P) is enforceable, and the judgment of the lower court must be affirmed.

▶ ANALYSIS

Perhaps the most significant distinction between gifts and trusts is that the former is ineffective without delivery. Almost any type of property, tangible or intangible, may be the subject of a gift or a trust. When interests in property not yet in existence are involved, however, the donor or trustor must make a present and irrevocable transfer of his interest in the property to be acquired. If the donor or trustor retains any interest in the future property or maintains any control over its distribution, the gift or trust will likely be deemed ineffective. Virtually every Anglo-American jurisdiction recognizes and applies this rule.

Quicknotes

ASSIGNMENT A transaction in which a party conveys his or her entire interest in property to another.

CONSIDERATION Value given by one party in exchange for performance, or a promise to perform, by another party.

LICENSEES Persons known to an owner or occupier of land, who come onto the premises voluntarily and for a specific purpose although not necessarily with the consent of the owner.

Clark v. Campbell

Parties not identified.

N.H. Sup. Ct., 82 N.H. 281 (1926).

NATURE OF CASE: Will contest.

FACT SUMMARY: The trustees of the estate were directed to give decedent's personal effects to the friends they knew she wished to receive them.

RULE OF LAW
Where the beneficiaries of a noncharitable trust cannot adequately be determined, the trust fails.

FACTS: Decedent left her personal property to her trustees in trust to "make disposal by way of memento . . . to such of my friends as they, my trustees, shall select." Decedent further stated that her trustees were familiar with her friends and her wishes. Heirs alleged that the trust was void for lack of definite beneficiaries or ascertainable standards to identify them.

ISSUE: Must there be a definite beneficiary of a trust or ascertainable standards for determining the identity of beneficiaries?

HOLDING AND DECISION: (Snow, J.) Yes. To be valid, a trust must have an identifiable beneficiary, or there must be adequate standards provided under the trust instrument for their identification in the future. "Friends" is too indefinite a class of beneficiaries. Appointment of property by the trustee could not be opposed, in most cases, since the permissible class is too vague for the court to determine whether the distribution was proper. The trust therefore fails, and the trustee holds for the taker under the will.

ANALYSIS

The attorney general of the state administers charitable trusts and can protect against trustee abuses. Therefore, charitable trusts will not fail for lack of a definite beneficiary. *Harrington v. Pier*, 105 Wis. 485. Personal wishes conveyed to the trustee by the testator are not sufficient to render an otherwise indefinite description of beneficiaries definite. *Olliffe v. Wells*, 130 Mass. 221.

■=■

Quicknotes

CESTUI QUE TRUST   Beneficiary; the party for whose benefit a trust is established.

UNJUST ENRICHMENT   The unlawful acquisition of money or property of another for which both law and equity require restitution to be made.

■=■

In re Searight's Estate

Department of taxation (P) v. Executor (D)

Ohio App. 9th Dist., 87 Ohio App. 417 (1950).

NATURE OF CASE: Appeal from probate decision.

FACT SUMMARY: The testator, by will, left $1,000 to his executor (D) to pay another to care for his dog for the rest of the dog's life, and the probate court found it was a valid honorary trust.

🏛 RULE OF LAW
An "honorary trust" is valid where it is for a valid purpose and the trustee accepts the testator's wishes, even though there is no beneficiary who can enforce the trust.

FACTS: The testator, by will, left $1,000 to his executor (D) to pay Florence Hand $0.75 per day to care for his dog for the rest of the dog's life. The probate court found that it was a valid "honorary trust."

ISSUE: Is an "honorary trust" valid where it is for a valid purpose and the trustee accepts the testator's wishes, even though there is no beneficiary who can enforce the trust?

HOLDING AND DECISION: (Hunsicker, J.) Yes. Normally, attempts to create a trust where there is no ascertainable beneficiary will fail, but an exception permits an "honorary trust" to survive. The requirements are that the trust have some legal purpose and that the trustee accepts the wishes of the testator. Here, the testator attempted to further no illegal purpose but rather a worthy one, and Florence accepted the dog and the responsibilities of care. The transfer into trust does not violate the rule against perpetuities since there is only $1,000 plus accumulated interest involved, which, at $0.75 per day, would be exhausted within 5 years. (The R.A.P. requires the transfer to vest within a life or lives in being plus twenty-one years.) Affirmed.

▶ ANALYSIS

Most jurisdictions do not recognize "honorary trusts." But no jurisdiction recognizes such a trust where the testator "requests" or "hopes" that the trustee will perform the stated tasks in the purported trust instrument. This would be an aleatory suggestion which the trustee could ignore while keeping the transfer into trust for his own benefit. It would then be void due to no affirmative trust intent.

Quicknotes

CHARITABLE TRUST A trust that is established for the benefit of a class of persons or for the public in general.

RULE AGAINST PERPETUITIES The doctrine that a future interest that is incapable of vesting within twenty-one years of lives in being at the time it is created is immediately void.

Olliffe v. Wells

Family of deceased (P) v. Executor (D)

Mass. Sup. Jud. Ct., 130 Mass. 221 (1881).

NATURE OF CASE: Action to have legacy of estate residue declared lapsed and to have property distributed among heirs at law and next of kin.

FACT SUMMARY: Testatrix devised residue of estate to the executor with an instruction to distribute it, according to his discretion, so as to carry out the testatrix's preexpressed wishes.

🏛 RULE OF LAW
Where a will upon its face shows that the devisee takes the legal title only and not the beneficial interest, and the trust is not sufficiently defined by the will to take effect, the equitable interest goes by way of resulting trust to the heirs or next of kin as property of the deceased not disposed of by his will.

FACTS: Testatrix left a will, and after giving various legacies, she devised to Wells (D), the named executor, the residue of the estate, which the executor (D) was empowered to distribute in such manner as in his discretion was best calculated to carry out the wishes of the testatrix as expressed to him. In an action by the heirs (P) and next of kin (P) of the testatrix to have the executor (D) distribute the residue to them, the executor (D) claimed that, prior to her death, the testatrix orally instructed him to give the residue to charities.

ISSUE: Where a will, on its face, gives legal title but not any beneficial interest to a devisee, and there is no express trust indicated, will a resulting trust arise in favor of heirs or next of kin?

HOLDING AND DECISION: (Gray, C.J.) Yes. The purported trust in favor of the charities did not appear on the face of will; therefore, it cannot be established by extrinsic evidence. Thus, the executor (D) only has discretion in the manner of distribution; he cannot choose the beneficiaries. Since the trust cannot be carried out, the bequest falls within the residue of the estate and goes to the heirs (P) and next of kin (P). If the charities had been expressly named, they could have enforced the trust against the executor (D), who received only a legal title, and no beneficial interest, in the devise.

▶ ANALYSIS

Where a testamentary trust fails for any reason, the assets that were to be a part of that trust must still be distributed. In some instances, the testator's will may provide for the distribution of such assets. But if no contingent provision was prepared, the assets must pass intestate. This has resulted, in some cases, in the assets going to heirs or next of kin specifically excluded by the testator. A statement by a testator, in his will, that certain individuals are not to share in his estate does not constitute a testamentary scheme.

◼▬◼

Quicknotes

DEVISEE A person upon whom a gift of real or personal property is conferred by means of a testamentary instrument.

EXTRINSIC EVIDENCE Evidence that is not contained within the text of a document or contract but which is derived from the parties' statements or the circumstances under which the agreement was made.

RESIDUARY ESTATE That portion of the estate which remains after all the estate has been distributed through the satisfaction of all claims and is conditional upon something remaining after the claims on the testator's estate are satisfied.

◼▬◼

Marsman v. Nasca

Wife of beneficiary (P) v. Trustee (D)

Mass. App. Ct., 30 Mass. App. 789, 573 N.E.2d 1025 (1991).

NATURE OF CASE: Appeal from judgment imposing constructive trust for breach of trust.

FACT SUMMARY: Because Farr (D), as trustee of Cappy Marsman's trust, did not inquire into Cappy's financial circumstances, Cappy was forced to give up the house he lived in as a means of solving his financial difficulties.

RULE OF LAW
Where a trust gives the trustee a discretionary power to pay amounts of the principal for the comfortable support and maintenance of a beneficiary, the trustee has a duty to inquire into the financial resources of that beneficiary so as to recognize his needs.

FACTS: Sara Marsman set up a trust that provided for her husband, Cappy, after her death. Farr (D), as trustee, had discretionary power to pay out amounts of the principal as he deemed advisable but failed to adequately explain that power to Cappy. Because Cappy was denied access to the principal, financial difficulties caused him to transfer his house to Sara's daughter, Sally, and her husband, Marlette (D), reserving a life estate for himself. After Cappy's death, Marlette (D), now sole owner due to Sally's death, told Margaret (P), Cappy's second wife, to vacate the premises. Margaret (P) brought an action in the probate court, which held that Farr (D) had breached his duty to inquire into Cappy's finances. Marlette (D) was ordered to convey the house to Margaret (P), and Farr (D) was ordered to reimburse Marlette (D) for upkeep expenses. Marlette (D) and Farr (D) appealed.

ISSUE: Where a trust gives the trustee a discretionary power to pay amounts of the principal for the comfortable support and maintenance of a beneficiary, does the trustee have a duty to inquire into the financial resources of that beneficiary so as to recognize his needs?

HOLDING AND DECISION: (Dreben, J.) Yes. Where a trust gives the trustee a discretionary power to pay amounts of the principal for the comfortable support and maintenance of a beneficiary, the trustee has a duty to inquire into the financial resources of that beneficiary so as to recognize his needs. A life beneficiary is to be maintained in accordance with his normal standard of living. Had Farr (D) met his duties either of inquiry or of distribution under the trust, Cappy would not have lost his home. Sally and Marlette (D) cannot be charged as constructive trustees of the prop-

erty, but the payments of principal that would have made it possible for Cappy to keep the house can be deemed to be a constructive trust in favor of his estate. Vacated and remanded for a determination of the amount to be paid Cappy's estate from the trust.

▌ ANALYSIS

Here, Farr (D) was directed by the trust agreement to pay Cappy enough for his "comfortable support," yet Farr (D) failed to do so. Prudence and reasonableness are the standard of conduct for trustees of a discretionary trust. However, a desire to save for a beneficiary's future medical needs does not warrant a persistent policy of miserliness toward those beneficiaries.

Quicknotes

CONSTRUCTIVE TRUST A trust that arises by operation of law whereby the court imposes a trust upon property lawfully held by one party for the benefit of another, as a result of some wrongdoing by the party in possession so as to avoid unjust enrichment.

DISCRETIONARY TRUST A trust pursuant to which the trustee is authorized to make decisions regarding the investment of the trust funds and the distribution of such funds to beneficiaries.

EXCULPATORY CLAUSE A clause in a contract relieving one party from liability for certain unlawful conduct.

TENANCY BY THE ENTIRETY The ownership of property by a husband and wife whereby they hold undivided interests in the property with right of survivorship.

Scheffel v. Krueger

Creditor (P) v. Trust beneficiary (D)

N.H. Sup. Ct., 782 A.2d 410 (2001).

NATURE OF CASE: Appeal of dismissal of trustee process action.

FACT SUMMARY: Scheffel (P) was awarded a judgment against Krueger (D) and attempted to reach trust assets of which Krueger (D) was the beneficiary.

🏛 RULE OF LAW
Spendthrift trust assets are not reachable by tort creditors even when the beneficiary's conduct constitutes a criminal act, unless the beneficiary is also the settlor or the assets were fraudulently transferred to the trust.

FACTS: Scheffel (P) was awarded damages in a tort action against Krueger (D) for his sexual assault of her minor child and subsequent broadcast of the act over the Internet. Scheffel (P) sought an attachment of Krueger's (D) beneficial interest in the Kyle Krueger Irrevocable Trust (trust). The trust was established by Krueger's (D) grandmother and its terms direct the trustee to pay all of the net income from the trust to Krueger (D) at least quarterly, or more frequently if he requests. The trustee is also authorized to pay any of the principal to Krueger (D) if in the trustee's sole discretion the funds are necessary for the maintenance, support and education of Krueger (D). Krueger (D) cannot touch the principal until 2016 and is prohibited from making any voluntary or involuntary transfers of his interest in the trust. The trust specifically provides that the trust proceeds cannot be assigned or given to creditors or reached by any legal or equitable process in satisfaction of any debt or liability prior to its receipt by Krueger (D). Scheffel (P) filed a trustee process action against Citizens Bank NH (D), the trustee defendant. Citizens (D) argued that the spendthrift provision barred the claim and moved to release the attachment and dismiss the claim. The Superior Court ruled that under *RSA* 564:23 (1997), the spendthrift provision is enforceable and dismissed Scheffel's (P) trustee process action. Scheffel (P) appealed.

ISSUE: Did the legislature intend *RSA* 564:23 to shield the trust assets from tort creditors, especially when the beneficiary's conduct constituted a criminal act?

HOLDING AND DECISION: (Duggan, J.) Yes. The legislature did intend *RSA* 564:23 to shield trust assets from tort creditors, even when the beneficiary's conduct constitutes a criminal act, unless the exceptions apply. According to *RSA* 564:23 a spendthrift trust is enforceable unless the beneficiary is also the settlor or the assets were fraudulently transferred to

the trust. In the present case, neither of these exceptions applies. Moreover, the trust instrument is a valid spendthrift trust because it contains a provision which does not allow the beneficiary to transfer his right to future payments, and a creditor shall not be able to subject the beneficiary's interest to the payment of its claim. Furthermore, the statute plainly states that a creditor of a beneficiary shall not be able to subject the beneficiary's interest to the payment of its claim. Therefore, the legislature did not intend that a tort creditor should be exempted from a spendthrift provision. Since the legislature did make two other exemptions, we must presume that no others were intended. In addition, no rule of public policy is available to overcome the statutory rule. The legislature has enacted a statute repudiating the public policy exception sought by Scheffel (P) and the court cannot question the wisdom of the statute. Lastly, the trust's purpose, to provide for Krueger's support, maintenance, and education, may still be fulfilled while Krueger (D) is incarcerated and after he is released, therefore the trust should not be terminated. Affirmed.

▶ ANALYSIS

This case is a prime example of how a spendthrift trust can be used not only as an estate planning tool, but can also protect beneficiaries from creditors. The reason the judgment creditors in *Wilcox v. Gentry* were able to garnish the payments from the trust and the creditor was not able to do so in the present case was because the trust in *Wilcox* was a discretionary trust with no spendthrift clause. Unlike in New Hampshire where the present case occurred, in certain jurisdictions spendthrift trusts cannot protect beneficiaries from creditors in some situations. For example, in *Bacardi v. White* disbursements from a spendthrift trust could be garnished to enforce judgments for alimony.

QUICKNOTES

SPENDTHRIFT TRUST A trust formed for the beneficiary's support, but with restrictions imposed so as to safeguard against the beneficiary's abuse.

Federal Trade Commission v. Affordable Media, LLC

Agency (P) v. Telemarketing business (D)

179 F.3d 1228 (9th Cir. 1999).

NATURE OF THE CASE: Appeal of finding of civil contempt for failure to repatriate funds.

FACT SUMMARY: The Andersons (D), a married couple on trial for their part in a fraudulent telemarketing scheme, had established an irrevocable trust under the jurisdiction of the Cook Islands. When ordered by the court to repatriate the funds in the trust, the Andersons (D) asserted that under the terms of the trust, they were unable to comply. The court found them in civil contempt.

🏛 RULE OF LAW
A party who is a protector for an offshore trust of which he is a beneficiary cannot assert an impossibility defense with regard to his ability to repatriate the trust's assets.

FACTS: The Andersons (D) organized a telemarketing scheme in which they sold investors the rights to profits from products sold on late-night television. The products included such questionable items as a water-filled dumbbell and a talking pet tag. The Andersons (D) appeared to be perpetrating a Ponzi scheme in which earlier investors are paid by later investors' investments until there are no more investors. The Federal Trade Commission (FTC) (P), upon hearing about the Andersons' (D) business practices, filed a complaint with the United States District Court for the District of Nevada, charging the Andersons (D) with violating the Federal Trade Commission Act and the Telemarketing Sales Rule. Upon a motion filed by the FTC (P), the court issued an ex parte temporary restraining order against the Andersons (D). Subsequent to two days of hearings, the court entered a preliminary injunction, incorporating the provisions of the temporary restraining order. The temporary restraining order and the preliminary injunction required the Andersons (D) to repatriate whatever assets that were being held for their benefit outside the country. Earlier, the Andersons (D) had created an irrevocable trust under the jurisdiction of the Cook Islands. Under the terms of the trust, the Andersons (D) were named co-trustees along with AsiaCiti Trust Limited (AsiaCiti), a company licensed under the laws of the Cook Islands to conduct trustee services. Further, the provisions of the trust stated that under "an event of duress," AsiaCiti could remove the Andersons (D) as co-trustees. The Andersons (D) were also protectors of the trust. When the Andersons (D) notified AsiaCiti that they were under court order to repatriate the funds in the trust, AsiaCiti informed them that the temporary restraining order was an "event of duress."

Hence, they were told, they were being removed as co-trustees. Consequently, the Andersons (D) would not have access to the funds to repatriate them. The district court found the Andersons (D) in civil contempt because they had not repatriated the trust's assets, nor had they provided an accounting of the trust's assets. The court continued the hearing several times to allow the Andersons (D) to purge themselves of their contempt. The Andersons (D) indicated that it was impossible for them to comply with the court's order because they did not have control of the trust. Ultimately, the court ordered them taken into custody. The Andersons (D) appealed the issuance of the preliminary injunction and the court's finding them in contempt.

ISSUE: May a party who is a protector of an offshore trust of which he is a beneficiary assert an impossibility defense with regard to repatriating the trust's assets?

HOLDING AND DECISION: (Wiggins, J.) No. A party who is a protector of an offshore trust of which he is a beneficiary may not assert an impossibility defense with regard to repatriating the trust's assets. Here, the Andersons (D) had created an offshore trust to put the trust's assets beyond the jurisdiction of the United States. However, the Andersons (D) retained control over the trust's assets by naming themselves protectors. The Andersons' (D) powers as protectors are not solely negative ones. They have affirmative powers to appoint new trustees. Hence, the anti-duress provisions are subject to the Andersons (D) as protectors. Therefore, the Andersons (D) could force a foreign trustee to repatriate the assets. Therefore, they cannot avail themselves of the impossibility defense. Affirmed.

▶ ANALYSIS

Some offshore trusts provide protectors with only negative powers. Such protectors might have the power only to veto trustee decisions. Other protectors' powers are not subject to anti-duress provisions. Since the Andersons could appoint new trustees, they had the power to appoint ones who would comply with the court order and repatriate the trust's funds.

■═■

QUICKNOTES

IRREVOCABLE TRUST A trust that is not capable of being revoked after it is established.

■═■

In re Trust of Stuchell

Life-income beneficiary (P) v. Court (D)

Or. Ct. App., 104 Or. App. 332, 801 P.2d 852 (1990).

NATURE OF CASE: Appeal from a dismissal of a petition to modify a trust.

FACT SUMMARY: A life-income beneficiary (P) of a trust sought court approval of an agreement to modify the trust, allowing it to continue if her mentally retarded son survived her since a direct distribution to him would impact his ability to qualify for public assistance.

🏛 RULE OF LAW

A trust may be terminated if all of the beneficiaries agree, none of the beneficiaries is under a legal disability, and the trust's purposes would not be frustrated by doing so.

FACTS: Stuchell established a testamentary trust with his granddaughter (P) as one of two surviving life-income beneficiaries. On the death of the last income beneficiary, the remainder was to be distributed equally to the granddaughter's (P) four children or to their lineal descendants. One of those children, Harrell, was mentally retarded and unable to live independently without assistance. If the remainder were distributed directly to Harrell, he would no longer qualify for public assistance. Thus, his mother (P) requested that the court approve an agreement made by the other income beneficiary and remaindermen. The court dismissed the petition for modification. The granddaughter (P) appealed.

ISSUE: May a trust be terminated if all of the beneficiaries agree, none of the beneficiaries is under a legal disability, and the trust's purposes would not be frustrated by doing so?

HOLDING AND DECISION: (Buttler, J.) Yes. A trust may be terminated if all of the beneficiaries agree, none of the beneficiaries is under a legal disability, and the trust's purposes would not be frustrated by doing so. However, in this case, the granddaughter (P), relying on Restatement (Second) of Trusts § 167(1) (1959), urged the court to extend the rule to permit modification. However, comment b to that section states that the court will not permit or direct the trustee to deviate from the terms of the trust merely because such deviation would be more advantageous to the beneficiaries than compliance. Here, the only purpose of the proposed amendment is to make the trust more advantageous to the beneficiaries. The most obvious advantage would be to the three remaindermen who have consented to the amendment. Since there is no authority for a court to approve the proposed modification, the trial court did not err in dismissing the petition. Affirmed.

▶ ANALYSIS

By its terms, the Restatement's rule applies only to the termination of a trust under very limited circumstances. Section 167(1) of the Restatement allows a court to permit the trustee to deviate from the terms of a trust if circumstances not known or anticipated by the settlor would defeat the purposes of the trust. The court noted that even if the Restatement rule were to be adopted as the law in Oregon, the limitation imposed by the comment would preclude permitting the proposed amendment.

Quicknotes

LIFE-INCOME BENEFICIARY A person who is the recipient of income generated by certain property for the duration of the person's life, the remainder of which is to pass on to another individual upon the income beneficiary's death.

REMAINDER BENEFICIARY A person who is to receive property that is held in trust after the termination of a preceding income interest.

In re Estate of Brown

Beneficiary (P) v. Court (D)

Vt. Sup. Ct., 148 Vt. 94, 528 A.2d 752 (1987).

NATURE OF CASE: Appeal from judgment terminating trust.

FACT SUMMARY: The lifetime beneficiaries (P) of Brown's trust petitioned the court (D) to terminate the trust.

> 🏛 **RULE OF LAW**
> An active trust may not be terminated, even with the consent of all the beneficiaries, if a material purpose of the settlor remains to be accomplished.

FACTS: Andrew Brown died after transferring his entire estate into a trust. The trust income and principal were to be used to provide an education for the children of his nephew, Woolson Brown. After that purpose was accomplished, the trust income and principal were to be used for the care and maintenance of Woolson and his wife so that they could live in the style they were accustomed. At their death, the remainder was to pass to Woolson's children. The trustee complied with the terms of the trust by using the proceeds for the education of Woolson's children and applying the proceeds to benefit Woolson and his wife after the education purpose was completed. Woolson and his wife petitioned the probate court for termination of the trust, arguing that the sole remaining purpose of the trust was to maintain their lifestyle and that the distribution of the assets was necessary to accomplish this purpose. The remaindermen, Woolson's children, filed consents to the proposed termination. The probate court denied Woolson's petition to terminate, and Woolson appealed. The superior court reversed, concluding that the only material trust purpose, the education of the children, had been accomplished. The trustee appealed.

ISSUE: May an active trust be terminated, even with the consent of all the beneficiaries, if a material purpose of the settlor remains to be accomplished?

HOLDING AND DECISION: (Gibson, J.) No. An active trust may not be terminated, even with the consent of all the beneficiaries, if a material purpose of the settlor remains to be accomplished. Here, the termination cannot be compelled because a material purpose remains to be accomplished. The trust instrument had two purposes. First, it provided for the education of Woolson's children. It is clear that the educational purpose of the trust was achieved. The second purpose was the assurance of lifelong income for the beneficiaries through the discretion of the trustee. The trustee has to use all the income and such part of the principal as is necessary for this purpose. This purpose would be defeated if termination of the trust were allowed. Reversed.

▶ *ANALYSIS*

Some courts will allow the termination of a testamentary trust by a compromise agreement between the beneficiaries and heirs entered into soon after the testator's death. In one case, the court allowed such a compromise regardless of whether a material purpose of the trust was defeated by the trust's termination (*Budin v. Levy*, 343 Mass. 644, 180 N.E. 2d 74 (1982)).

■═■

Quicknotes

LIFE-INCOME BENEFICIARY A person who is the recipient of income generated by certain property for the duration of the person's life, the remainder of which is to pass on to another individual upon the income beneficiary's death.

REMAINDERMAN A person who has an interest in property to commence upon the termination of a present possessory interest.

RESIDUARY BENEFICIARIES Person specified pursuant to will to receive the portion of the estate remaining following distribution of the assets and the payment of costs.

SUPPORT TRUST A trust pursuant to which the trustee is authorized to only distribute such funds as are required for the support of the beneficiary.

SPENDTHRIFT TRUST A trust formed for the beneficiary's support, but with restrictions imposed so as to safeguard against the beneficiary's abuse.

■═■

Building Flexibility into Trusts: Powers of Appointment

Quick Reference Rules of Law

Irwin Union Bank & Trust Co. v. Long

Bank (D) v. Ex-wife of trustee (P)

Ind. Ct. App., 160 Ind. App. 509, 312 N.E.2d 908 (1974).

NATURE OF CASE: Appeal from order allowing execution on a portion of a trust corpus.

FACT SUMMARY: The trial court ordered that four percent of the trust corpus of a trust held as trustee by Philip Long was subject to execution in favor of his ex-wife (P).

 RULE OF LAW
A power of appointment that is unexercised may not be reached by a creditor of the trustee.

FACTS: Philip Long was made the trustee of a trust by his mother and was granted a right of appointment of four percent of the trust corpus. Long was subsequently sued by his wife, Victoria Long (P), for divorce, and a judgment in the amount of $15,000 was entered in favor of Victoria (P). Victoria (P) then filed an action to execute upon 4 percent of the trust corpus in which she contended that, because Philip had a right of appointment with regard to this percentage of the trust, it could be reached by his creditors. The trial court, over the objections of Irwin Union Bank and Trust Co. (D) that an unexercised right of appointment cannot be reached by creditors, issued the writ of execution. Union Bank (D) appealed.

ISSUE: May an unexercised right of appointment be reached by creditors of the trust deed?

HOLDING AND DECISION: (Lowdermilk, J.) No. An unexercised right of appointment may not be reached by creditors of the beneficiary. In the absence of a statute, the unexercised general right of appointment cannot be reached by creditors, as to hold to the contrary would allow creditors to force the exercise of said power upon the beneficiary. If the beneficiary chooses not to exercise the power, creditors cannot force him to do so. Where the power is a special power, the appointee derives no benefit therefrom, and, therefore, it cannot be reached by his creditors. As a result, the trial court erred in granting the writ of execution. Reversed.

▶ ANALYSIS

The principal case is cited and followed by the Restatement Second Property donative transfers. The basis upon which this case is determined is that a right of appointment is not property. Because the beneficiary does not derive any benefit from it, it cannot be attached by his creditors. The power of appointment is personal to the beneficiary and therefore cannot be alienated. As a result, it lacks a fundamental element of the concept of property and therefore cannot be attached.

Quicknotes

POWER OF APPOINTMENT Power, created by another person in connection with a gratuitous transfer (often in trust), residing in a person (as trustee or otherwise) to affect the disposition or distribution of the property.

TRUST CORPUS The aggregate body of assets placed into a trust.

Sterner v. Nelson

Parties not identified.

Neb. Sup. Ct., 210 Neb. 358, 314 N.W.2d 263 (1982).

NATURE OF CASE: Appeal from decision construing a will.

FACT SUMMARY: While Oscar Wurtele in his will gave his wife all of his property "absolutely with full power in her to make such disposition of said property as she may desire," he thereafter provided that whatever was left in her hands on her death would vest in his foster daughter, Sterner.

🏛 RULE OF LAW
Where there is a grant, devise, or bequest to one in general terms only, expressing neither fee nor life estate, and there is a subsequent limitation over what remains at the first taker's death, if there is also given to the first taker an unlimited and unrestricted power of absolute disposal, express or implied, the grant, devise, or bequest to the first taker is construed to pass a fee simple interest, and the attempted subsequent limitation over is void.

FACTS: By the terms of his will, Oscar Wurtele bequeathed all of his property to his wife "absolutely with full power in her to make such disposition of said property as she may desire." He also therein provided that whatever of such property remained in his wife's possession at the time of her death would vest in his foster daughter, Sterner. An action was instituted that involved construction of these provisions, and the court granted a summary judgment to the effect that the wife had been granted a fee simple absolute.

ISSUE: Is an attempted limitation over, following a gift which is in fee with full power of disposition and alienation, void?

HOLDING AND DECISION: (Krivosha, C.J.) Yes. Where there is a grant, devise, or bequest to one in general terms only, expressing neither fee nor life estate, and there is a subsequent limitation over of what remains at the first taker's death, if there is also given to the first taker an unlimited and unrestricted power of absolute disposal, express or implied, the grant, devise, or bequest to the first taker is construed to pass a fee simple interest. The attempted subsequent limitation over, following a gift which is in fee with full power of disposition and alienation, is void. A testator simply cannot give an estate in fee simple by clear and concise language and subsequently diminish or destroy the devise by use of other language. That is the rule to apply here. Affirmed.

▶ ANALYSIS

The rule highlighted in this case is known as the rule of repugnancy. It has not been spared criticism and has been tagged as an arbitrary rule that serves no public policy, results in a complete frustration of the legitimate intention of the testator, and is productive of enormous amounts of unnecessary litigation. See C. J. Vanderbilt's dissent in *Fox v. Snow*, 6 N.J. 12 (1950).

Quicknotes

FEE SIMPLE ABSOLUTE An estate in land characterized by ownership of the entire property for an unlimited duration and by absolute power over distribution.

JOINT TENANCY An interest in property whereby a single interest is owned by two or more persons and created by a single instrument; joint tenants possess equal interests in the use of the entire property and the last survivor is entitled to absolute ownership.

Seidel v. Werner

Trustees (P) v. Wife of trust beneficiary (D)

N.Y. Sup. Ct., 81 Misc. 2d 220, 364 N.Y.S.2d 963 (1975).

NATURE OF CASE: Suit seeking declaratory judgment to determine who was entitled to a portion of a trust.

FACT SUMMARY: Trustees (P) of Werner's trust sought a declaratory judgment to determine who was entitled to the share in which Steven Werner was a life beneficiary and over which he had a testamentary power of appointment.

> ## RULE OF LAW
> A promise to appoint a given sum to persons who would take in default of appointment is not the same as a release of the power of appointment.

FACTS: Trustees (P) of a trust established by Werner sought a declaratory judgment to dermine who was entitled to one-half of the principal of the trust. This was the share in which Steven was a life beneficiary and had a testamentary power of appointment. Steven's children, Anna (P) and Frank (P), claimed that Steven's share of the trust remainder on the basis of a Mexican divorce which incorporated by reference and approved a separation agreement entered into by Steven and Anna (P) and Frank's (P) mother, Harriet (P). The agreement promised not to revoke a will in which Steven exercised his testamentary power of appointment over his share of the trust for the benefit of his children. After the divorce, however, Steven executed a will that exercised his testamentary power of appointment in favor of this third wife, Edith (D). Anna (P), Frank (P) and Harriet (P) argued that Steven's agreement should be considered a release of his power of appointment and, as such, Anna (P) and Frank (P) should take on default of appointment.

ISSUE: Is a promise to appoint a given sum to persons who would take in default of appointment the same as a release of the power of appointment?

HOLDING AND DECISION: (Silverman, J.) No. A promise to appoint a given sum to person who would take in default of appointment is not the same as a release of the power of appointment. Part of the separation agreement was a contract to exercise a testamentary power of appointment not presently exercisable, which is invalid under New York Statute EPTL 10-5.3(a). EPTL 10-5.3(b), however, permits a donee of a power to release the power. If that release conforms with EPTL 10-9.2, then it prevents the donee from exercising the power. Under the terms of the trust, if Steven failed to

exercise his power of appointment, then Anna (P) and Frank (P) would take the property subject to Steven's power of appointment. The parties did not intend a release of the power of appointment. On the contrary, the agreement expressly contemplated an exercise of the power of appointment. Nor was the substantial effect of the promised exercise the same as that of a release or failure to exercise the power. Under the separation agreement, the power was to be exercised entirely for the benefit of Anna (P) and Frank (P) and would be held in trust until they reached twenty-one. If, however, Anna (P) and Frank (P) failed to qualify to take the principal, then the principal would go to Steven's estate. Steven's failure to exercise the power would have resulted in the property going to all of Steven's children absolutely and in fee. Judgment for Edith (D).

ANALYSIS

As mentioned in Seidel EPTL 10-5.3(b) permits a donee to release his power of appointment. After Seidel was decided, the section was amended. The revised section allows a "donee of a power of appointment which is not presently exercisable to release his power pursuant to 10-9.2 or to make the power, after release, an imperative power, except that where the donor designated persons or a class to take in default of the donee's exercise of the power, a release with respect to appointive property must serve to benefit all those designated as provided by the donor."

■──■

QUICKNOTES

INCORPORATION BY REFERENCE The reference to another document in a writing, stating that the secondary writing should be considered as part of the principal document.

POWER OF APPOINTMENT Authority granted to an individual, pursuant to a will or deed, to make decisions regarding the selection of persons to receive the income or property of an estate following the death of the grantor.

■──■

Beals v. State Street Bank & Trust Co.

Parties not identified.

Mass. Sup. Jud. Ct., 367 Mass. 318, 326 N.E.2d 896 (1975).

NATURE OF CASE: Petition for instructions on distribution of a portion of a trust.

FACT SUMMARY: In an action seeking instructions on how a portion of a trust should be distributed, State Street Bank, as trustee, sought to determine if a power of appointment could be considered to have been exercised by a general residuary clause in a will.

RULE OF LAW

The fact that there has been a prior partial release of a general power does not obviate the application of that rule of construction which presumes that a general residuary clause in a will exercises a general power of appointment.

FACTS: As trustee, State Street Bank & Trust Co. sought instructions on how a portion of a trust should be distributed. The central question was whether Isabella had, by means of the general residuary clause in her will, exercised the power of appointment she had been given by the trust. While she had been given a general power of appointment, Isabella had subsequently partially released her general power of appointment. She released it "to the extent that such power empowers me to appoint to any one other than one or more of the . . . descendants [surviving me] of Arthur Hunnewell."

ISSUE: Does the fact that there has been a prior partial release of a general power obviate the application of that rule of construction which presumes that a general residuary clause in a will exercises a general power of appointment?

HOLDING AND DECISION: (Wilkins, J.) No. The fact that there has been a prior partial release of a general power of appointment does not obviate the application of that rule of construction which presumes that a general residuary clause in a will exercises a general power of appointment. That same rule has not been extended to special powers. In this case, the power initially given to Isabella was a power of general appointment that she reduced to what was effectively a special power by her own actions, which themselves amounted to treating the property as her own. Thus, the rule applicable to special powers is not on point, and it must be considered that Isabella exercised her power of appointment by means of the general residuary clause in her will.

ANALYSIS

A majority of jurisdictions take the approach adopted in the following provision of the Uniform Probate Code (§ 2-610): "A general residuary clause in a will, or a will making general disposition of all of the testator's property, does not exercise a power of appointment held by the testator unless specific reference is made to the power or there is some other indication of intention to include the property subject to the power." Since this case was heard, Massachusetts has adopted the Uniform Probate Code.

Quicknotes

POWER OF APPOINTMENT Power, created by another person in connection with a gratuitous transfer (often in trust), residing in a person (as trustee or otherwise) to affect the disposition or distribution of the property.

RESIDUARY CLAUSE (OF WILL) A clause contained in a will disposing of the assets remaining following distribution of the estate.

Loring v. Marshall

Parties not identified.

Mass. Sup. Jud. Ct., 396 Mass. 166, 484 N.E.2d 1315 (1985).

NATURE OF CASE: Declaratory judgment action seeking determination of proper testamentary beneficiary.

FACT SUMMARY: Morse, beneficiary with power of appointment under Hovey's will, declined to appoint his portion of the proceeds to all potential appointees.

🏛 RULE OF LAW
When a beneficiary with powers of appointment appoints his portion of will proceeds to less than the full class of potential appointees, the nonappointed class members will take the beneficiary's share if the appointees are deceased.

FACTS: Hovey's will made Morse a beneficiary thereof. The will, by its terms, gave Morse the power to appoint the proceeds of the testamentary trust created by the will to his wife and issue. Morse, in his will, left only a nominal legacy to his son and appointed his trust proceeds to his wife. Following the wife's death, both Morse's son and the trust's remaindermen made claim to the trust principal.

ISSUE: When a beneficiary with powers of appointment appoints his portion of will proceeds to less than the full class of potential appointees, will the nonappointed class members take the beneficiary's share if the appointees are deceased?

HOLDING AND DECISION: (Wilkins, J.) Yes. When a beneficiary with powers of appointment appoints his portion of will proceeds to less than the full class of potential appointees, the nonappointed class members will take the beneficiary's share if the appointees are deceased. If a will does not contain a provision creating a gift in default of appointment, it is presumed that a testator wished testamentary proceeds to remain within the class of beneficiaries and their potential appointees. If the beneficiaries and actual appointees no longer live, then the law presumes that the testator intended the proceeds to pass to the remaining potential appointees. Here, Morse's son is a living potential appointee, and, therefore, the proceeds are properly his. The cause is remitted to the trial court for a determination of executor and counsel fees.

▌ ANALYSIS

The position taken by the court here appears to be the majority rule. It can be found in the Restatement, 2d of Property, Donative Transfers § 24.2. Essentially, the rule implies a donative intent on the part of the testator to the entire class of named potential appointees. This presumption can be rebutted, if the will so provides.

━■━

Quicknotes

INCOME BENEFICIARY A person who is the recipient of income generated by certain property.

POWER OF APPOINTMENT Power, created by another person in connection with a gratuitous transfer (often in trust), residing in a person (as trustee or otherwise) to affect the disposition or distribution of the property.

REMAINDERMAN A person who has an interest in property to commence upon the termination of a present possessory interest.

━■━

CHAPTER 10

Construction of Trusts: Future Interests

Quick Reference Rules of Law

In re Estate of Gilbert

Executor (P) v. Beneficiary (D)

N.Y. Surrogate Ct., 156 Misc. 2d 379, 592 N.Y.S.2d 224 (1992).

NATURE OF CASE: Motion to declare trust beneficiary's renunciation void.

FACT SUMMARY: When Lester (D), who was a beneficiary of discretionary trusts under his father's will, renounced his interest in the estate, the executor (P) moved to declare the renunciation premature and therefore invalid.

🏛 **RULE OF LAW**
A beneficiary of a discretionary trust may renounce his interest in the disposition.

FACTS: Decedent was survived by a wife and four children. By will, he created two sets of discretionary trusts for the benefit of his children. One son, Lester (D), who had taken a vow of poverty, renounced his share of the estate. Lester (D) was a discretionary income beneficiary of two testamentary trusts. The executor (P) filed a motion to declare Lester's (D) renunciation void. The executor (P) argued that Lester (D) possessed no current property interest to renounce and that a renunciation could be made only after the trustees exercised their discretion to distribute income or principal.

ISSUE: May a beneficiary of a discretionary trust renounce his interest in the disposition?

HOLDING AND DECISION: (Roth, S.) Yes. A beneficiary of a discretionary trust may renounce his interest in the disposition. Renunciations are governed by statute. A statutory renunciation need not relate to specific property. Instead, the statute merely requires the disclaimant to renounce his or her interest in a trust. Therefore, a beneficiary of a discretionary trust may renounce his interest in the disposition. Assuming, arguendo, that in order to be effective the renounced interest must be in the nature of property, Lester's (D) renunciation would still be valid. Courts have recognized the right of a trust beneficiary to compel a distribution of funds where trustees abuse their discretion in refusing to make distributions. Therefore, a beneficiary who has the right to compel trustees to distribute trust property under certain circumstances arguably has a current interest that could be deemed property for the purpose of an effective renunciation. Motion denied.

▶ *ANALYSIS*

As important as the attempt to effectuate the intent of the testator is, an individual cannot be compelled to accept an inheritance against his will. Furthermore, once an individual has disclaimed or renounced his interest in an estate, most states by statute presume the individual to have predeceased the testator. This is preferable to attempting to litigate the testator's intent had he known the individual would renounce.

Quicknotes

CONTINGENT REMAINDER A remainder limited to a person not in being, not certain or ascertained, or so limited to a certain person that his right to the state depends upon some contingent event in the future.

DISCRETIONARY TRUST A trust pursuant to which the trustee is authorized to make decisions regarding the investment of the trust funds and the distribution of such funds to beneficiaries.

GUARDIAN AD LITEM Person designated by the court to represent an infant or ward in a particular legal proceeding.

RENUNCIATION The abandonment of a right or interest.

Clobberie's Case

Parties not identified.

Ct. Ch., 2 Vent. 342, 86 Eng. Rep. 476 (1677).

NATURE OF CASE: Suit seeking an order construing a bequest.

FACT SUMMARY: Money was bequeathed to a woman at her age of twenty-one years or day of marriage, to be paid with interest. The woman died without marrying or attaining the age of twenty-one.

🏛 RULE OF LAW
If a bequest is "to be paid" at the happening of a certain event, the money passes to the estate of the beneficiary even if he dies before the contingency occurs.

FACTS: Money was bequeathed to a certain woman at her age of twenty-one years or day of marriage, to be paid to her with interest. She died prior to marrying or attaining the age of twenty-one. It was argued that the bequest, instead of lapsing, should pass to the executor of her estate.

ISSUE: If a bequest is "to be paid" at the occurrence of a stated event, but the beneficiary dies before the contingency occurs, does the bequest pass to his estate?

HOLDING AND DECISION: (Finch, L.C.) Yes. If a bequest is "to be paid" at the happening of a certain event, the money passes to the estate of the beneficiary even if he dies before the contingency occurs. In this case, money was bequeathed to the woman at her age of twenty-one years or her wedding day and was to be paid with interest. Thus, upon her death, the money passed to the executor of her estate. If the money had merely been bequeathed at the occurrence of a stated event, the death of the beneficiary prior to its occurrence would have resulted in the loss of the money. But, where the money is "to be paid" at the occurrence of the designated event, it shall pass to the beneficiary's executors despite his failure to survive until the event takes place. Therefore, the bequest to the woman in this case passes to her executor.

▮ ANALYSIS

The rule in *Clobberie's Case* has long perplexed the student of future interests in property. The rule causes significantly different consequences to ensue from the most minute differences in language. The rule in *Clobberie's Case* is still applied by some courts, although it has been repeatedly modified and updated. Perhaps no case of comparable succinctness has enjoyed notoriety equivalent to that earned by *Clobberie's Case*.

Quicknotes

BEQUEST A transfer of property that is accomplished by means of a testamentary instrument.

Dewire v. Haveles

Parties not identified.

Mass. Sup. Jud. Ct., 404 Mass. 274, 534 N.E.2d 782 (1989).

NATURE OF CASE: Action to declare rights in a residuary trust.

FACT SUMMARY: Haveles contended the testator failed to manifest a contrary intent in his will that a right of survivorship should apply to a gift to the grandchildren; therefore, Dewire was not entitled to share in her father's legacy.

🏛 RULE OF LAW
Members of a class pursuant to a class gift are joint tenants with rights of survivorship unless a contrary intent is expressed in the will.

FACTS: Thomas Dewire died, leaving a widow, a son named Thomas Jr., and three grandchildren. He placed his estate in a residuary trust, the income payable to his widow for life and on her death to his son, his widow, and Thomas Jr.'s children. After the testator's death, Thomas Jr. had three more children by a second wife and then died. He was survived by six children, including Thomas III, who served as trustee until his death. Thomas III left one child, Jennifer. Upon Thomas III's death, an action was brought to determine the rights of the remaining grandchildren in the estate. Haveles contended that Jennifer, the issue of Thomas III, could not take a share of the grandchildren's gift, as a class gift had been created for the grandchildren with a right of survivorship. Jennifer contended that a contrary intent was manifested in the original will to supersede the joint tenancy, and, therefore, she was entitled to her father's share.

ISSUE: Does a class gift create a joint tenancy with right of survivorship in the absence of contrary intent expressed in the will?

HOLDING AND DECISION: (Wilkins, J.) Yes. A class gift creates a joint tenancy with right of survivorship unless a contrary intent is expressed in the will. Because the testator must have intended for the income of the trust to be paid out during the term of its existence, the only logical recipients of that income would be the issue, by right of representation, of deceased grandchildren, the same group of people who would take the trust assets upon termination of the trust. As a result, a contrary intent to the right of survivorship was expressed in the will, and, therefore, Jennifer was entitled to her father's share of the estate.

▶ ANALYSIS

The court as a side issue indicated that this will violated the rule against perpetuities. This most confusing and ancient rule has been the source of many will invalidations. However, a will in this case survived under the general policy that upholds the balance of a will when one part is invalid. Had a joint tenancy been recognized in this case, Thomas III's share would have passed to his remaining cousins rather than passing on to his daughter.

Quicknotes

CLASS GIFT A gift to a group of unspecified persons whose number, identity, and share of the gift will be determined sometime in the future.

JOINT TENANCY An interest in property whereby a single interest is owned by two or more persons and created by a single instrument; joint tenants possess equal interests in the use of the entire property and the last survivor is entitled to absolute ownership.

RIGHT OF SURVIVORSHIP Between two or more persons, such as in a joint tenancy relationship, the right to the property of a deceased passes to the survivor.

RULE AGAINST PERPETUITIES The doctrine that a future interest that is incapable of vesting within twenty-one years of lives in being at the time it is created is immediately void.

Estate of Woodworth

Parties not identified.

Cal. Ct. App., 18 Cal. App. 4th 936 (1993).

NATURE OF CASE: Appeal from an order rejecting a claim to the remainder of a testamentary trust.

FACT SUMMARY: Because the trustee was uncertain as to whether the heirs at law of the ancestor named to take the remainder of the Woodworth trust should be determined at the date of the named ancestor's death or at the date of the life tenant's death, the trustee petitioned the court for that determination.

RULE OF LAW
The identity of heirs entitled to trust assets must be determined at the date of death of the named ancestor who predeceased the life tenant, not at the date of death of the life tenant.

FACTS: Woodworth's will distributed a portion of his estate outright to his wife, Mamie Barlow Woodworth, with the balance to be administered as a testamentary trust with Mamie as the life tenant. Upon her death, any remainder of the trust estate was to go to Woodworth's sister, Elizabeth Plass, or to her heirs at law, if she no longer survived. Elizabeth died before Mamie but was survived by her husband, Ray Plass, a niece, and a nephew. Ray also died before Mamie, leaving the residue of his estate to the Regents of the University of California. At Mamie's death, the trustee petitioned the probate court as to the date for determining who would receive the distribution of the trust estate. Concluding that the heirs must be determined as of the date of death of the life tenant, Mamie, the court ordered the assets distributed to Elizabeth's niece and nephew. The regents appealed.

ISSUE: Must the identity of heirs entitled to trust assets be determined at the date of death of the named ancestor who predeceased the life tenant, not at the date of death of the life tenant?

HOLDING AND DECISION: (DiBiaso, J.) Yes. The identity of heirs entitled to trust assets must be determined at the date of death of the named ancestor who predeceased the life tenant, not at the date of death of the life tenant. Nothing in the language of the other provisions of the decree of distribution revealed Woodworth's intent or desire. The general rule favoring early vesting was well-established long before Woodworth died. Nothing in the decree forecloses the possibility that Woodworth took into account the fact that Raymond Plass might succeed to a portion of the trust remainder. Moreover, the fact that the university, an entity, is not a rela-

tive of Elizabeth Plass or one of her heirs at law is not material. In addition, the language of the decree does not contain any expression of futurity in the description of the ancestor's heirs. Therefore, the regents have a claim to the assets of the trust. Reversed.

▶ ANALYSIS

In the absence of any firm indication of testamentary intent, the rules of construction must be implemented in order to insure uniformity and predictability in the law. This is preferable to carrying out a court's ad hoc sense of what is, with perfect hindsight, acceptable in a particular set of circumstances. Here, at the time of Elizabeth Plass' death, her "heir at law" was her husband, Ray.

Quicknotes

DEFEASIBLE FEE SIMPLE ESTATE A fee simple interest in land that is subject to being terminated upon the happening of a future event.

LIFE ESTATE An interest in land measured by the life of the tenant or a third party.

LIFE TENANT An individual whose estate in real property is measured either by his own life or by that of another.

REMAINDER An interest in land that remains after the termination of the immediately preceding estate.

TESTAMENTARY TRUST A trust created by will and only effective after the grantor's death, since the assets that comprise the corpus of the trust are assumed to vest at that time.

Lux v. Lux

Parties not identified.

R.I. Sup. Ct., 109 R.I. 592 (1972).

NATURE OF CASE: Will contest.

FACT SUMMARY: Lux left the residue of her estate to her grandchildren, some of whom might not be born until after her death.

 RULE OF LAW
A class gift should be closed when all existing beneficiaries attain a specific age.

FACTS: Lux's will left her estate to her husband, who predeceased her. A clause in her will provided for this contingency, leaving the residue of her estate to her grandchildren, per capita. Lux's real property was to be sold when the youngest grandchild reached age twenty-one. Until then, the property was to be held for their benefit. Lux had five grandchildren alive at her death. Lux's son informed the court that he intended to have more children. An attorney was appointed to act as guardian for the present grandchildren, and another attorney was appointed to represent the interest of persons having an interest who are not presently known or lives in being. The dispute centered on whether the gift of the real property was in fee or in trust, when the class gift was to close, and when the heirs were to be determined. Since there is a presumption that a person remains fertile, it is conceivable that the class might have to remain open until the son's death.

ISSUE: Should a class be closed when all of the existing beneficiaries have obtained the stated age?

HOLDING AND DECISION: (Kelleher, J.) Yes. First, we find that Lux did not intend to give the grandchildren a fee simple interest in the property. No specific words of art are necessary to create a testamentary trust. Nor is it necessary that all possible beneficiaries be named or a trustee appointed. Where, as here, when all of the facts are viewed in their entirety, it is clear that a trust was intended and that the class should be closed and the members determined, we find that when the youngest existing child reaches twenty-one, the class should be deemed closed. While there is a presumption of continued fertility, we adopt the rule of convenience, which requires that a class be closed when all existing members meet the testator/trustor's requirements. If necessary, the trustee may dispose of the real property and use the proceeds to purchase productive trust assets. Any income earned from trust assets shall be distributed in equal shares to all class members since this is the normal presumption when the trust instrument does not specify that the income is to be accumulated.

▶ ANALYSIS

The rule of convenience adopted in *Lux* only applies to situations involving the division of a specific sum to the class members. It does not apply where a fixed sum is to be awarded to each member of the class, i.e., a per capita gift. Where there is a per capita gift, the class closes at the date of death of the testator. Of course the rule of convenience is merely an aid to construction, and it will yield to an expression of the testate's intent. *Earle's Estate*, 369 Pa. 521 (1951).

Quicknotes

CLASS GIFT A gift to a group of unspecified persons whose number, identity, and share of the gift will be determined sometime in the future.

RESIDUARY CLAUSE (OF WILL) A clause contained in a will disposing of the assets remaining following distribution of the estate.

TESTAMENTARY TRUST A trust created by will and only effective after the grantor's death, since the assets that comprise the corpus of the trust are assumed to vest at that time.

CHAPTER 1

Trust Duration and The Rule Against Perpetuities

Quick Reference Rules of Law

Dickerson v. Union National Bank of Little Rock

Son (P) v. Executor (D)

Ark. Sup. Ct., 268 Ark. 292, 595 S.W.2d 677 (1980).

NATURE OF CASE: Appeal of dismissal of action seeking to invalidate a testamentary trust.

FACT SUMMARY: A will created a testamentary trust that was to continue until the death of the testator's sons and a possible widow of one son.

🏛 RULE OF LAW
An instrument creating a trust naming as beneficiaries children of an unnamed spouse violates the rule against perpetuities.

FACTS: Dickerson's will created a trust. Named as beneficiaries were Dickerson's two sons and the widow, unnamed, of one of the sons. After the death of the last of these three individuals, the trust was to end, and the principal was to be distributed to the issue of the three. Cecil (P), one of the sons, brought an action to nullify the will as violative of the rule against perpetuities. The Chancery Court held the will valid and dismissed. Cecil (P) appealed.

ISSUE: Does an instrument creating a trust naming as beneficiaries children of an unnamed spouse violate the rule against perpetuities?

HOLDING AND DECISION: (Smith, J.) Yes. An instrument creating a trust naming as beneficiaries children of an unnamed spouse violates the rule against perpetuities. Under the rule, any remainder must vest within twenty-one years of a life in being at the time of the death of the testator. A common pitfall is the "born widow," a problem existing here. This widow conceivably could be born after the testator's death, which would exclude her from being a measuring life. She might live longer than twenty-one years after her husband's death, which would cause any vesting of proceeds in her children after her death to violate the rule. While this is only a theoretical scenario, a mere theoretical possibility is all that is needed to invoke the rule. Reversed.

▶ ANALYSIS

The present action was brought several years after the probate proceeding on the will. The rule against perpetuities objection was not made at the probate proceeding. The trial court, besides holding the rule inapplicable on the merits, held this a waiver. The state supreme court disagreed, ruling that the rule was not waivable.

Quicknotes

HOLOGRAPHIC WILL A will that is handwritten by the testator or testatrix.

RES JUDICATA The rule of law that a final judgment by a court precludes subsequent litigation between the parties regarding the same cause of action.

RULE AGAINST PERPETUITIES The doctrine that a future interest that is incapable of vesting within twenty-one years of lives in being at the time it is created is immediately void.

In re Trust of Wold

Parties not identified.

N.J. Sup. Ch. Div., 708 A.2d 787 (1998).

NATURE OF CASE: Request for determination about validity of a proposed trust.

FACT SUMMARY: Elaine Wold proposed to extend and continue a trust set up by her father in 1944 pursuant to a revised law on the Rule Against Perpetuities.

RULE OF LAW
The extension of a trust through the power of appointment is valid and subject to the revised Rule Against Perpetuities, which allows a "wait and see" approach.

FACTS: Johnson, one of the principal heirs of the Johnson & Johnson company, established a trust in 1944 with his children as beneficiaries. The trustees were directed during the lifetime of Wold to pay her as much income as was in her best interest. Wold was given the power to direct the proceeds of the trust in her last will and testament. The trust was set up with maximum flexibility to meet the needs of Johnson's children. Wold sought to continue and extend the trust for the benefit of her granddaughters through a testamentary appointment. However, the Rule Against Perpetuities in effect in 1944 prevented the creation of a property interest that would not necessarily vest within 21 years after the death of a living person. In 1991, New Jersey revised this rule to allow a "wait and see" approach, which does not invalidate the property interest if it actually vests within 90 years of its creation. Wold requested that a court rule on whether her proposed extension of the trust would comply with the law.

ISSUE: Is the extension of a trust through the power of appointment valid and subject to the revised Rule Against Perpetuities, which allows a "wait and see" approach?

HOLDING AND DECISION: (Hamlin, J.) Yes. The extension of a trust through the power of appointment is valid and subject to the revised Rule Against Perpetuities, which allows a "wait and see" approach. Generally, the donor of a special power intends that the donee have the same discretion in making an appointment as the donor had in making the original disposition. Thus, it is clear that Wold is entitled to continue and extend the 1944 trust through the power of appointment provided by Johnson. Under the common law Rule Against Perpetuities, an interest that was not certain to vest within the specified period was considered invalid. Under the revised rule, an interest that would have violated the old rule is valid if the interest in fact vests within 90 years of creation. It becomes invalid only if it remains in existence and

does not vest within that time period. This new statutory rule is not to be applied retroactively but only to interests created after the law was in effect. In the present case, even though Wold's power of appointment was created in 1944, it is the new rule that applies to her proposed nonvested interest created by the exercise of that power after the new rule became law, but measured from the trust creation in 1944.

ANALYSIS

The end result of this decision is that trust will come to an end 90 years after its creation in 1944. The chief reason that Wold sought to extend the trust was to avoid certain taxes. In 1999, New Jersey once again changed the Rule Against Perpetuities, this time permitting perpetual trusts under certain circumstances.

Quicknotes

PERPETUAL TRUST A trust that is to continue for as long as its purpose is necessary.

POWER OF APPOINTMENT An authority granted by one person to another to affect the disposition or distribution of an estate or income in connection with a gratuitous transfer.

CHAPTER 12

Charitable Trusts

Quick Reference Rules of Law

Shenandoah Valley National Bank v. Taylor

Trustee (D) v. Heir-at-law (P)

Va. Sup. Ct. App., 192 Va. 135, 63 S.E.2d 786 (1951).

NATURE OF CASE: Suit challenging validity of a testamentary trust.

FACT SUMMARY: A testator created a perpetual trust, the income of which was to be paid in equal shares to each student in a particular grade school just before Christmas and Easter. Although the payments were purportedly for educational purposes, an heir challenged the validity of the trust.

🏛 **RULE OF LAW**
For a charitable trust to be valid, it must provide relief for poor or needy or otherwise benefit or advance the social interest of the community.

FACTS: The terms of the testator's will left the bulk of his $86,000 estate to the Shenandoah Valley National Bank (D), as trustee, to administer a perpetual trust. The trust funds were to be invested and the income was to be paid to all the first-, second-, and third-grade students in a particular local grade school. The payments were to be made in equal shares to each student directly and were to be distributed just before the Christmas and Easter vacations. The trust directed that the money so distributed was to be used by each student for the furtherance of his or her education. Although the testator had no children or other close relative, Taylor (P), a distant relative and heir, brought suit challenging the validity of the trust as not being charitable and therefore violative of the rule against perpetuities.

ISSUE: For a charitable trust to be valid, must it provide relief for the poor or needy or otherwise benefit or advance the social interest of the community?

HOLDING AND DECISION: (Miller, J.) Yes. There is a fundamental difference between a trust that is charitable and one that is benevolent. A benevolent trust, while it may be praiseworthy, is a private enterprise and is subject to the rule against perpetuities. A charitable trust is public and is not subject to the rule. For a perpetual charitable trust to be valid, it must provide relief to the poor or needy or otherwise benefit or advance the social interest of the community. The most common examples of such interests include the relief of poverty, the advancement of education, the advancement of religion, the promotion of health, and governmental or municipal purposes. The keystone is the accomplishment of a purpose which is beneficial to the community. While the testator's scheme would surely delight the recipients, there is no way that the stated purpose of educational advancement can be assured. The timing of the payments and the ages of the children practically assure the opposite. This trust cannot be classified as charitable, and as it violates the rule against perpetuities, it must fail.

▶ **ANALYSIS**

A perpetual charitable trust may validly be directed toward a small ascertainable group so long as the recipients are qualified as to actual need. Such provisions as providing for the support of needy widows and children of the deceased ministers of a particular church have been upheld for example. Where no need test is applied, the group benefited must be needy by definition, such as young seamstresses (upheld at a time before minimum wage laws). Generally, the larger the class, the less strict the application of the needs test.

■━■

Quicknotes

CHARITABLE TRUST A trust that is established for the benefit of a class of persons or for the public in general.

PERPETUAL TRUST A trust which is to continue for as long as its purpose is necessary.

RULE AGAINST PERPETUITIES The doctrine that a future interest that is incapable of vesting within twenty-one years of lives in being at the time it is created is immediately void.

TESTAMENTARY TRUST A trust created by will and only effective after the grantor's death, since the assets that comprise the corpus of the trust are assumed to vest at that time.

■━■

In re Neher

Parties not identified.

N.Y. Ct. App., 279 N.Y. 370, 18 N.E.2d 625 (1939).

NATURE OF CASE: Appeal from the denial of a petition for a decree to construe and reform a charitable gift.

FACT SUMMARY: When Red Hook Village (P) found it did not have the resources to establish and maintain a hospital on property willed to the village (P) by Ella Neher, the village (P) petitioned the court for permission to establish instead an administration building designated as the "Herbert Neher Memorial Hall."

🏛 RULE OF LAW
Where a will gives real property for a general charitable purpose, the gift may be reformed cy pres when compliance with a particular purpose grafted on to the general purpose is impracticable.

FACTS: Ella Neher's will gave her home in Red Hook Village (P) to the village (P) to be used as a memorial to the memory of her husband. She further directed that the property be used as a hospital to be known as the "Herbert Neher Memorial Hospital." The village (P) accepted the gift but later discovered that it was without the resources necessary to establish and maintain a hospital on the property. Furthermore, a modern hospital in a neighboring village adequately served the needs of both communities. Instead, the village (P) petitioned the court for leave to erect and maintain a building for the administration purposes of the village (P) to be designated as the "Herbert Neher Memorial Hall." The court denied the petition. The appellate division affirmed. The village (P) appealed.

ISSUE: Where a will gives real property for a general charitable purpose, may the gift be reformed cy pres when compliance with a particular purpose grafted on to the general purpose is impracticable?

HOLDING AND DECISION: (Loughran, J.) Yes. Where a will gives real property for a general charitable purpose, the gift may be reformed cy pres when compliance with a particular purpose grafted on to the general purpose is impracticable. When taken as a whole, the true construction of the paragraph outlining the gift in Neher's will is that the paramount intention was to give the property for a general charitable purpose rather than a particular charitable purpose. Neher's gift to the village (P) did not specify what sort of medical or surgical care should be provided. The direction grafted on to the general gift, that the property be used for a hospital, may be ignored where, as here, the village (P) finds

compliance with that direction impracticable due to a lack of resources. Reversed.

▶ ANALYSIS

Application of the doctrine of cy pres allows a charitable trust to continue rather than fail. The doctrine's application occurs where the court can discern a primary general charitable intent and where the altered charitable purpose falls within the general charitable intent of the settlor. Such reformation allows the donor's general intent to be carried out even where changes unforeseen by the settlor eliminate the need for the gift's original intended use.

■■■

Quicknotes

CHARITABLE TRUST   A trust that is established for the benefit of a class of persons or for the public in general.

DOCTRINE OF CY PRES   Equitable doctrine applied in order to give effect to an instrument, which would be unlawful if enforced strictly, as close to the drafter's intent as possible without violating the law.

■■■

Smithers v. St. Luke's-Roosevelt Hospital Center

Estate's administratrix (P) v. Charitable donee (D)

N.Y. App. Div., 281 A.D.2d 127 (2001).

NATURE OF CASE: Appeal from dismissal for lack of standing of suit to enforce terms of a charitable gift.

FACT SUMMARY: Smithers (P), administratrix for her husband's estate, brought suit to enforce the terms of a charitable gift made by her deceased husband to St. Luke's Roosevelt Hospital Center (the "Hospital") (D). The gift was restricted for the purpose of establishing an alcoholism center and maintaining it in its own building.

RULE OF LAW

The estate of a donor of a charitable gift has standing to sue the donee to enforce the terms of the gift.

FACTS: Mr. Smithers made a $10 million gift to St. Luke's Roosevelt Hospital Center (the "Hospital"), which was dedicated for the purpose of establishing an alcoholism rehabilitation center. One of the conditions of the gift was that the center be housed in its own building, separate from the Hospital (D). Years of investigations by the state Attorney General (D) revealed that the Hospital (D) had misappropriated funds from the charitable fund to fund other hospital projects. The Attorney General (D) entered into an agreement with the Hospital (D) whereby the Hospital (D) agreed to not use gift funds for any purpose other than to benefit the center and to return to the gift fund proceeds from any sale of the building in which the center was housed. Smithers (P), administratrix for Mr. Smithers' estate, filed a claim against both the Hospital (D) and Attorney General (D) to enforce the terms of her deceased husband's gift She sought an accounting of the funds of the gift, and also sought an injunction preventing the Hospital (D) from selling the building in which the rehabilitation center was housed, or, alternatively, preventing disbursement of the funds from the sale. The Hospital (D) and Attorney General (D) moved to dismiss, and the trial court granted the defendants' motions. The appellate division granted review.

ISSUE: Does the estate of a donor of a charitable gift have standing to sue the donee to enforce the terms of the gift?

HOLDING AND DECISION: (Ellerin, J.) Yes. The estate of a donor of a charitable gift has standing to sue the donee to enforce the terms of the gift. Standing to enforce the terms of charitable gifts is not exclusive to the Attorney General (D). Here, Smithers (P) is bringing her suit as administratrix of her husband's estate, not on her own behalf or on behalf of the center's beneficiaries. Therefore, the general rule barring beneficiaries from suing charitable corporations has no application here. The donor of a charitable gift is in a better position than the Attorney General (D) to be vigilant and, if he or she is so inclined, to enforce his or her own intent. Mr. Smithers was the founding donor of the Smithers Center, which he established to carry out his vision of "first class alcoholism treatment and training." In his agreement with the Hospital (D) he reserved to himself the right to veto the Hospital's (D) project plans and staff appointments for the Smithers Center. He and Smithers (P) remained actively involved in the affairs of the Smithers Center until his death, and she thereafter. During his lifetime, when Mr. Smithers found that his intent was not carried out by the Hospital (D), he decided not to donate the balance of the gift. It was only when the Hospital (D) expressly agreed to the various restrictions imposed by Mr. Smithers that he completed the gift. The Hospital's (D) subsequent unauthorized deviation from the terms of the completed gift commenced during Smithers's lifetime and was discovered shortly after he died. To hold that, in her capacity as her late husband's representative, Smithers (P) has no standing to institute an action to enforce the terms of the gift is to contravene the well-settled principle that a donor's expressed intent is entitled to protection and the longstanding recognition under state law of standing for a donor such as Mr. Smithers. There is thus a need for co-existent standing for the Attorney General (D) and the donor; the Attorney General's (D) interest in enforcing gift terms is not necessarily congruent with that of the donor. Therefore, the distinct but related interests of the donor and the Attorney General (D) are best served by continuing to accord standing to donors to enforce the terms of their own gifts concurrent with the Attorney General's (D) standing to enforce such gifts on behalf of the beneficiaries thereof. Reversed on the standing issue.

DISSENT: (Friedman, J.) When a charitable gift is made, without any provision for a reversion of the gift to the donor or his heirs, the interest of the donor and his heirs is permanently excluded. Accordingly, in the absence of a right of reverter, the right to seek enforcement of the terms of a charitable gift is restricted to the Attorney General (D). This general rule is consistent with the common-law rule, and with the approach found in the Restatement (Second) of Trusts. Such a rule is necessary to avoid "vexatious litigation" by parties who

Continued on next page.

do not have a tangible stake in the outcome of the litigation. It is uncontroverted that the estate was not the donor of the gift. Thus, even if pure donor standing were recognized (as the majority concludes), this could not be a basis for granting standing to Mr. Smithers's estate. To the extent that Mr. Smithers may have had standing based upon his right to exercise discretionary control over the gift, i.e., via the right to appoint key staffing positions, that right was personal to him, abated upon his death, and did not devolve to his estate.

▶ *ANALYSIS*

The approach taken by the court in this case finds support in the Uniform Trust Code, which provides that "[t]he settlor of a charitable trust, among others, may maintain a proceeding to enforce the trust." Of course, this can be interpreted as granting only a personal right in the donor, not one that survives the donor's death.

Quicknotes

CHARITABLE TRUST A trust that is established for charitable purposes.

DONEE A person to whom a gift is made.

DONOR A person who gives real or personal property or value.

Trust Administration: The Fiduciary Obligation

Quick Reference Rules of Law

Hartman v. Hartle

Daughter of testatrix (P) v. Executor (D)

N.J. Super. Ch. Div., 95 N.J. Eq. 123, 122 A. 615 (1923).

NATURE OF CASE: Bill in equity to set aside the sale of property by executors for fraud and illegality.

FACT SUMMARY: After an executor (D) indirectly sold property to his wife, who resold the property at a substantial profit, Hartman (P), testatrix's daughter, filed a complaint to set aside the original sale.

RULE OF LAW
A trustee breaches his duty of loyalty to the beneficiaries when he engages in self-dealing.

FACTS: Testatrix died leaving five children. She named her two sons-in-law (D) as executors. In her will, testatrix expressly directed the executors (D) to sell her real estate. The proceeds were to be divided equally among her children. However, part of the real estate was sold for $3,900 to Geick, a son of the testatrix. He bought it for his sister, Dieker, the wife of one of the executors (D). Dieker then resold the property for $5,500. Hartman (P), a second daughter of the testatrix, filed a complaint to set aside the first sale for fraud and illegality. She contended that the sale of the property by the executors (D) to Dieker, the wife of one of them, without previous authority from the court, was illegal and void.

ISSUE: Does a trustee breach his duty of loyalty to the beneficiaries when he engages in self-dealing?

HOLDING AND DECISION: (Foster, V.C.) Yes. A trustee breaches his duty of loyalty to the beneficiaries when he engages in self-dealing. It is the settled law of this state that a trustee cannot purchase from himself at his own sale and that his wife is under the same disability, unless leave to do so has been previously obtained under an order of the court. In view of the fact that the property is now owned by innocent purchasers, a resale cannot be ordered, but as an alternative, Dieker and the executors (D) will be held to pay one-fifth of their profit on the resale to Hartman (P). Decree so ordered.

▶ ANALYSIS

Once it is shown that a trustee has engaged in self-dealing, the no-further-inquiry rule is triggered; the trustee will be liable for any profit realized, without inquiry by the court as to the trustee's good faith or the transaction's reasonableness. The trustee may assert two defenses—either that the self-dealing was approved by the settlor or was fully disclosed to the beneficiaries, who then gave their consent. The strict no-further-inquiry rule is justified by the fiduciary relationship between the trustee and the beneficiaries, which is held to a higher standard than arm's-length transactions.

Quicknotes

DUTY OF LOYALTY A director's duty to refrain from self-dealing or to take a position that is adverse to the corporation's best interests.

In re Rothko

Daughter of decedent (P) v. Executors of decedent's estate (D)

N.Y. Ct. App., 43 N.Y.2d 305, 372 N.E.2d 291, N.Y.S.2d 449 (1977).

NATURE OF CASE: Appeal from award of damages for breach of trust.

FACT SUMMARY: Kate Rothko (P), the decedent's daughter, contended that the three executors of the estate had violated their fiduciary duties by entering into contracts with businesses in which they had an interest and selling the decedent's paintings for less than their full value.

RULE OF LAW
A trustee must refrain from placing himself in a position where his personal interest or that of a third person does or may conflict with the interest of the beneficiaries.

FACTS: Mark Rothko, an abstract expressionist painter whose works through the years gained him an international reputation of greatness, died testate on February 25, 1970, leaving an estate consisting of 798 paintings of tremendous value. During a period of three weeks after the will was admitted to probate, the three executors, Reis (D), Stamos (D), and Levine (D), dealt with all 798 paintings. The executors agreed to sell to Marlborough A.G. (MAG), a Liechtenstein corporation, 100 of the paintings. The executors also consigned to Marlborough Gallery, Inc. (MNY) approximately 700 paintings. After Kate Rothko (P), the decedent's daughter, brought an action to remove the executors, it was established that Reis (D), in addition to being a coexecutor of the estate, was a director, secretary, and treasurer of MNY; that it was to the advantage of Stamos (D), as an aspiring artist, to curry favor with MNY; and that Levine (D), while not acting in self-interest or bad faith, nonetheless failed to exercise ordinary prudence in the performance of his fiduciary obligations since he was aware of the actual and potential conflicts of interests which existed. The trial court also held that the present value of the paintings was the proper measure of damages. All three executors and the two corporations then brought this appeal, contending, inter alia, that there was no breach of fiduciary duty since they had acted in good faith and the plan was fair and that the measure of damages should be based upon the value of the paintings at time of sale.

ISSUE: Must a trustee refrain from placing himself in a position where his personal interest or that of a third person may or does conflict with the interest of the beneficiaries?

HOLDING AND DECISION: (Cooke, J.) Yes. While a trustee is administering the trust or estate, he must refrain from placing himself in a position where his personal interest of that of a third person does or may conflict with the interest of the beneficiaries. The duty of loyalty imposed on the fiduciary prevents him from accepting employment from a third party who is entering into a business transaction with the trust or estate. An executor who knows that his coexecutor is committing breaches of trust and not only fails to exert efforts directed toward prevention but accedes to them is legally accountable even though he was acting on the advice of counsel. If the trustee is authorized to sell trust property but in breach of trust he sells it for less than he should receive, he is liable for the value of the property at the time of the sale less the amount which he received. The trustee may be held liable for appreciation damages if it was his or her duty to retain the property upon the theory that the beneficiaries are entitled to be placed in the same position they would have been in had the breach not consisted of a sale of property that should have been retained. Here, there is no doubt that Reis (D) and Stamos (D) had a conflict of interest regarding MNY or that Levine (D) knew of such conflict and ignored it. Further, Rothko (P) is entitled to appreciation damages due to the wrongful acts of the executors. Affirmed.

ANALYSIS

In addressing the issue of appreciation damages, Professor Scott states that: "If the trustee is guilty of a breach of trust in selling trust property for an inadequate price, he is liable for the difference between the amount he should have received and the amount which he did receive. He is not liable, however, for any subsequent rise in value of the property sold." See 3 Scott, Trust (3d ed.) § 208.6, pp. 1689–1690.

QUICKNOTES

CONFLICT OF INTEREST Refers to ethical problems that arise, or may be anticipated to arise, between an attorney and his client if the interests of the attorney, another client or a third party conflict with those of the present client.

DUTY OF LOYALTY A director's duty to refrain from self-dealing or to take a position that is adverse to the corporation's best interests.

Estate of Collins

Beneficiaries (P) v. Trustees (D)

Cal. Ct. App., 72 Cal. App. 3d 663, 139 Cal. Rptr. 644 (1977).

NATURE OF CASE: Appeal from an action for damages for breach of a trust.

FACT SUMMARY: Plaintiffs, beneficiaries under a testamentary trust, brought suit against Lamb (D) and Millikan (D), the trustees, alleging that they had improperly invested $50,000.

RULE OF LAW
The trustee is under a duty to the beneficiary to distribute the risk of loss by reasonable diversification of investments, unless under the circumstances it is prudent not to do so.

FACTS: The primary beneficiaries (P) under the Collins testamentary trust were his wife and children. The will authorized the trustees, Lamb (D) and Millikan (D), to purchase every kind of property or investment. It also provided that the trustees had absolute discretion in exercising the provisions of the trust. After probate, Lamb (D) and Millikan (D) had about $50,000 available for investment. Millikan's (D) clients included two real property developers, Downing and Ward. The trustees (D) learned that the developers wanted to borrow $50,000, which would be secured by a second trust deed to 9.38 acres of unimproved real property. This property was subject to a $90,000 first trust deed. The trustees (D) knew the property had been sold earlier for $107,000. However, they did not have the property appraised, relying instead on the word of the two real estate brokers in the area. In fact, when the trustees (D) made the loan, there were six notices of default and three lawsuits pending against the developers. After the developers declared bankruptcy, the trustees (D) became the owners of the property. Later, the holder of the first trust deed foreclosed, and the trust fund lost about $60,000. Several years later, the trustees (D) filed a petition for an order settling the account and discharging themselves. The beneficiaries (P) objected and requested that the trustees (D) be surcharged. The trial court ruled in favor of the trustees (D) and terminated the trust. The beneficiaries (P) appealed.

ISSUE: Are trustees under a duty to the beneficiary to diversify the trust investments?

HOLDING AND DECISION: (Kaus, J.) Yes. California relies on the prudent investor rule, which encompasses the following guidelines. First, the trustee is under a duty to the beneficiary to distribute the risk of loss by reasonable diversification of investments, unless under the circumstances

it is prudent not to do so. Second, ordinarily, second or other junior mortgages are not proper trust investments, unless taking a second mortgage is a reasonable method of settling a claim or making possible the sale of property. Third, in buying a mortgage for trust investment, the trust should give careful attention to the valuation of the property in order to make certain that his margin of security is adequate. This court thinks that the trustees, Lamb (D) and Millikan (D), violated every applicable rule. First, they failed totally to diversify the investments. Second, they invested in junior mortgages on unimproved real property and left an inadequate margin of security. As noted, the land had recently been sold for $107,000 and was subject to a first trust deed of $90,000. Thus, unless the land was worth more than $140,000, there was no margin of security at all. They did not have the land appraised. Thus, any assumption that there was a margin of security would have been little more than a guess. Third, the backup security obtained by them was no security at all. The builders pledged 20 percent of their stock, but the trustees (D) never obtained possession of the stock, placed it in escrow, or even had it legended. In conclusion, the evidence does not support the trial court's conclusion that the trustees (D) acted properly. Reversed.

▶ ANALYSIS

"Running throughout the disparate legal approaches to the regulation of risk is a consistent concern with one particular type of risk: the risk of loss. In addition to focusing solely on risk of loss, current regulation is limited to minimizing that risk on each particular security, rather than on the portfolio as a whole. In evaluating the investment of trust funds, the prudent man rule treats each investment separately. Losses in one investment cannot be set off against other investments, and each investment must stand or fall by itself." (The Regulation of Risky Investments, 83 Harv. L. Rev. 603, 616-621, 1970.)

In re Estate of Janes

Wife of testator (P) v. Trustee (D)

N.Y. Ct. App., 90 N.Y.2d 41, 681 N.E.2d 332, 659 N.Y.S.2d 165 (1997).

NATURE OF CASE: Appeal from award of damages for negligent retention of trust assets.

FACT SUMMARY: Mrs. Janes (P) argued that the trustee (D) appointed to oversee her husband's testamentary trusts violated its fiduciary duty to maintain a diversified portfolio of the trust's investments by retaining a majority of the assets in Kodak stock.

RULE OF LAW

A fiduciary, in executing his duties as trustee, is required to invest the assets of a trust as a prudent person would in the management of his own affairs.

FACTS: Rodney Janes, the testator, died in 1973 leaving an estate valued at $3.5 million. The estate held $2.5 million in stocks, 71 percent of which were shares in Eastman Kodak Company. Janes's will devised his estate to three trusts. The first trust was comprised of 50 percent of the estate, granting Mrs. Janes (P) the income for life and a general power of appointment as to the principal. Second, Janes created a charitable trust consisting of 25 percent of the assets of the estate. The remainder of his assets were placed in a trust designating income to Mrs. Janes (P) for life, and the remainder to the charitable trust. At the time of Janes's death, the Kodak stock was valued at $135 per share. By the end of 1973, however, the value of the shares had fallen to $109 per share. By 1978, the value of the stock had declined even further to $40 per share. The surrogate court held that the estate's trustee (D) had violated its fiduciary duty by retaining the Kodak stock and employed a "lost profits" measure of damages. The appellate division affirmed but modified the measure of damages used, concluding that the proper damages should be calculated as the difference between the stock's value at the time it should have been sold and its value when it was actually sold. Both parties appealed.

ISSUE: Does a trustee violate his fiduciary duty by failing to diversify the investment of trust assets?

HOLDING AND DECISION: (Levine, J.) Yes. A fiduciary, in executing his duties as trustee, is required to invest the assets of a trust as a prudent person would in the management of his own affairs. The trustee's predominate objectives must be the maintenance of the trust assets and the acquisition of a sufficient income. In determining whether the trustee has satisfied his duty to invest the trust assets prudently, the court must consider the attendant facts and circumstances.

This requires the court to examine the trustee's thoughts and actions in respect to each investment of the trust property, at the moment the act or omission occurred. While the court may not evaluate the trustee's decision based on the result of the investment, the court must necessarily consider the trustee's overall performance in managing the trust assets. The holding of a large percentage of the trust assets in one investment is prima facie evidence of imprudence. However, the individual investment must be examined in relation to several factors. These include the total value of the estate, relevant cost of living expenses, economic conditions, the beneficiaries' need, the asset's marketability, and potential tax liabilities. This requires the court to examine the individual investment in relation to the performance and circumstances of the trust as a whole. Here the trustee (D) failed to discharge his duties as would a prudent investor in the management of his own affairs. The appellate division was correct in setting damages as the amount of value lost to the trust by virtue of the improvident investment. This requires the court to determine the difference between what the value of the stock was on the date that it should have been sold, and the value of the stock when it was in fact sold or at the date of the accounting. Applying this formula to the present case, the proper measure of damages is $4,065,029. Affirmed.

ANALYSIS

The determination of the date and value at which the investment should have been sold presents a difficult issue for resolution by the court. The court states that such action should be taken within a "reasonable" time period. The discernment of what constitutes a "reasonable" time necessarily depends upon the facts and circumstances of the individual case, and is determined consistent with the prudent investor standard.

QUICKNOTES

CHARITABLE TRUST   A trust that is established for the benefit of a class of persons or for the public in general.

POWER OF APPOINTMENT   Power, created by another person in connection with a gratuitous transfer (often in trust), residing in a person (as trustee or otherwise) to affect the disposition or distribution of the property.

Dennis v. Rhode Island Hospital Trust Co.

Beneficiaries (P) v. Trustee (D)

744 F.2d 893 (1st Cir. 1984).

NATURE OF CASE: Appeal of certain orders in an action based on breach of fiduciary duty.

FACT SUMMARY: The bank (D) held onto certain real estate in a declining market, leaving a relatively small corpus for the remaindermen.

🏛 RULE OF LAW
A trustee who fails to unload trust assets that are declining in value may be liable to trust remaindermen.

FACTS: A testamentary trust created in 1920 was due to terminate in 1991. During the life of the trust, its income was to go to the testator's living issue; upon its termination, the principal was to go to the testator's then-living issue. The principal trust assets were three commercial buildings in downtown Providence, Rhode Island. From 1920 on, apart from a brief renaissance after World War II, the buildings' values decreased, although rents remained fairly high. The three buildings were sold in 1945, 1970, and 1979. Eventually, the two remaindermen brought an action against Rhode Island Hospital Trust Co. (D), alleging breach of fiduciary duty. The district court found the bank (D) to have improperly favored the income beneficiaries over the remaindermen by failing to unload income-producing but depreciating assets, and awarded a $365,000 surcharge. The bank (D) appealed.

ISSUE: May a trustee who fails to unload trust assets that are declining in value be liable to the trust remaindermen?

HOLDING AND DECISION: (Breyer, C.J.) Yes. A trustee who fails to unload trust assets that are declining in value may be liable to the trust remaindermen. A trustee is obligated to treat all beneficiaries impartially; he may not favor one class over another. A failure to abide by the principle may give rise to the aggrieved class. Here, the district court held that the bank (D) should have realized that the buildings, although generating good income, were declining in value to the detriment of the remaindermen. From this, the court was free to conclude that the bank (D) improperly favored the income beneficiaries over the remaindermen, and its holding was therefore appropriate. [The court reduced the damages to about $345,000 to not penalize the bank (D) to the extent that it did not outperform inflation.] Affirmed as modified.

▶ ANALYSIS

As this case shows, all beneficiaries are not created equally. Sometimes, there can be actual adversity between beneficiary classes. A trustee, to discharge his fiduciary duties, must sometimes walk a tightrope between the classes.

QUICKNOTES

FIDUCIARY DUTY A legal obligation to act for the benefit of another, including subordinating one's personal interests to that of the other person.

INCOME BENEFICIARY A person who is the recipient of income generated by certain property.

LIFE TENANT An individual whose estate in real property is measured either by his own life or by that of another.

REMAINDERMAN A person who has an interest in property to commence upon the termination of a present possessory interest.

Fletcher v. Fletcher

Beneficiary (P) v. Trustee (D)

Va. Sup. Ct., 480 S.E.2d 488 (1997).

NATURE OF CASE: Appeal from decision mandating opening of trust documents.

FACT SUMMARY: James Fletcher (P), the beneficiary of a trust, sought to compel Henry Fletcher (D) and the other trustees to reveal the entire contents of the trust document.

RULE OF LAW

Trustees have a duty to provide complete and accurate information as to the nature and amount of the trust property to the beneficiary of the trust.

FACTS: Elinor Fletcher executed a trust that upon her death provided for the establishment of three trusts benefiting James (P), Andrew, and Emily Fletcher. Henry Fletcher (D) and a bank were made trustees and given the discretion to pay income and principal to provide medical care to the beneficiaries. After Elinor died and the trust came into effect, James (P) filed suit against the trustees (D) requesting all the details about the trust. The trustees (D) provided only certain pages of the trust documents and claimed that Elinor wanted the terms to be kept confidential. The trustees (D) sought to dismiss the action on the basis that it did not state a claim. However, the trial court ruled that James (P) was entitled to see all the provisions of the trust agreement. The trustees (D) appealed.

ISSUE: Do trustees have a duty provide complete and accurate information as to the nature and amount of the trust property to the beneficiary of the trust?

HOLDING AND DECISION: (Compton, J.) Yes. Trustees have a duty to provide complete and accurate information as to the nature and amount of the trust property to the beneficiary of the trust. The beneficiary is the equitable owner of trust property. The trustee is the mere representative whose function is to attend to the safety of the trust property. This arrangement does not imply that the beneficiary is to be kept ignorant of the nature and details of the trust and its administration. Therefore, trustees have a duty to provide beneficiaries with this information at reasonable times. Although the terms of the trust may regulate the amount of information the trustee must give, the beneficiary is always entitled to such information as is reasonably necessary to enable enforcement of rights under the trust. In the present case, without access to the trust agreement James (P) has no basis upon which to scrutinize whether the trustees (D) are discharging their duty impartially and with reasonable care. Accordingly, the trustees (D) must disclose the information. Affirmed.

ANALYSIS

The court noted that the trustees (D) claimed that Elinor orally indicated a desire for confidentiality. However, there was no evidence submitted on this matter at the trial level to properly judge this claim. While the trustees (D) could still try to demonstrate this, the decision was fairly clear in indicating that James (P), as beneficiary, had broad rights to the information he was seeking.

Quicknotes

TRUSTEE A person who is entrusted to keep or administer property for the benefit of another.

National Academy of Sciences v. Cambridge Trust Co.

Remainderman (P) v. Bank (D)

Mass. Sup. Jud. Ct., Mass. 346 N.E.2d 879 (1976).

NATURE OF CASE: Appeal from a petition seeking revocation of seven decrees allowing the trustee's accounting.

FACT SUMMARY: The National Academy of Sciences (P), a remainderman under a trust, brought an action seeking revocation of seven court decrees allowing accounts of the Cambridge Trust Company (D), the trustee.

🏛 RULE OF LAW
Where the subject matter is one of fact in respect to which a person can have precise and accurate knowledge and he speaks as of his own knowledge and has no such knowledge, his affirmation constitutes constructive or technical fraud.

FACTS: The will of Troland left all of his real and personal property to be held in trust by the Cambridge Trust Company (D), with the net income to be paid to his wife, provided she did not remarry. On his wife's remarriage or death, the bank (D) was to transfer the trust and trusteeship to the National Academy of Sciences (P). The bank (D) paid income from the trust to the widow until her death in 1967. In 1945, the widow remarried without the bank's (D) knowledge. In 1968, the bank (D) brought a suit for recovery of amounts paid to the widow subsequent to the date of her marriage. In this litigation, the bank (D) recovered $41,000, from which it paid legal fees of $14,000. The total amount collected by the widow after her marriage was $106,000. The bank (D) presented this account, and it was allowed. Thereafter, the academy (P) brought an action seeking revocation of the bank's (D) account. The judge revoked the accounting and ordered restoration to the trusts of those amounts erroneously delivered to the decedent's widow. The appellate court affirmed, and the bank (D) appealed.

ISSUE: Where the subject matter is one of fact in respect to which a person can have knowledge and he speaks as of his own knowledge and has no such knowledge, does his affirmation constitute fraud?

HOLDING AND DECISION: (Reardon, J.) Yes. The principle is well settled that if a person makes a representation of fact as of his own knowledge and such representation is not true as to a subject matter susceptible of knowledge, if the party to whom it is made relies and acts upon it as true and sustains damage by it, it is fraud, for which the party making it is responsible. In this case, the marital status of Mrs.

Troland/Flynn was a fact susceptible of precise knowledge. The bank (D) made representations concerning this fact of its own knowledge when it had no such knowledge, and the academy (P) to whom the representations were made relied on them to its detriment. The bank (D) exerted no effort at all to ascertain if Mrs. Troland had remarried even to the extent of annually requesting a statement or certificate from her to that effect. Affirmed.

▶ ANALYSIS

In order to avoid expensive accountings, provisions are often inserted in a trust instrument providing that judicial accountings should be dispensed with and accounts rendered periodically to the adult income beneficiaries of the trust. In the case of testamentary trusts, a few courts have indicated that a testator will not be permitted to dispense with statutorily required accountings. (Bogert & Bogert, Trusts & Trustees, § 973, 2d ed. 1962). In the case of inter vivos trusts, which are not placed under judicial supervision by statutes, it would appear that a "no judicial accounting" provision does not contravene public policy.

Quicknotes

CONSTRUCTIVE FRAUD Breach of a duty at law or in equity that tends to deceive another to whom the duty is owed, resulting in damages.

FIDUCIARY DUTY A legal obligation to act for the benefit of another, including subordinating one's personal interests to that of the other person.

Wealth Transfer Taxation: Tax Planning

Quick Reference Rules of Law

Holtz's Estate v. Commissioner

Trustee (P) v. Commissioner (D)

U.S.T.C., 38 T.C. 37 (1962).

NATURE OF CASE: Appeal from imposition of gift tax.

FACT SUMMARY: Holtz's estate (P) disputed a determination by the Commissioner (D) that taxable gifts resulted from transfers to a trust that he established.

🏛 RULE OF LAW
If a trustee is free to exercise his unfettered discretion and there is nothing to impel or compel him to invade the corpus, the settlor retains a mere expectancy that does not make the gift of corpus incomplete, thus indicating that the settlor has abandoned dominion and control over the property.

FACTS: Holtz transferred funds to a trust by deed of trust in 1953, wherein Holtz was the settlor and the Land Title Bank and Trust Company was the trustee (P). The trust instrument provided that during the lifetime of the settlor the income should be paid to him and as much principal as the trustee (P) "may from time to time think is desirable for the welfare, comfort and support of the Settlor, or for his hospitalization or other emergency needs." At the settlor's death, the income of the trust would go to his wife if she survived him, as well as any of the principal that she might need in accordance with the trustee's (P) discretion. The trust was to terminate at the death of the survivor of the settlor and his wife, and the remaining principal was payable to the survivor's estate. Holtz transferred property worth $384,117 to the trust in 1953, and in 1955, he transferred an additional $50,000 in cash. The Commissioner (D) subsequently determined that as a result of these transfers, Holtz made taxable gifts that were subject to the appropriate gift tax. Holtz's estate (P) contested and claimed that the transfers were not completed gifts and not subject to a gift tax.

ISSUE: If a trustee is free to exercise his unfettered discretion and there is nothing to impel or compel him to invade the corpus, does the settlor retain a mere expectancy that does not make the gift of corpus incomplete?

HOLDING AND DECISION: (Drennan, J.) Yes. The rule generally is that if the trustee is free to exercise his unfettered discretion and there is nothing to impel or compel him to invade the corpus, the settlor retains a mere expectancy which establishes a completed gift to the corpus. However, where, as here, the trustee's (P) discretion is governed by some external standard that a court may apply in compelling

compliance with the conditions of the trust agreement and the trustee's (P) power to invade is unlimited, then the gift of corpus in unlimited. Since the trustee (P) had the unfettered power to use all of the corpus for the benefit of the settlor, it was entirely possible that the entire corpus might be distributed to the settlor during his lifetime with the result that no one other than the settlor would receive any portion thereof. As long as that possibility was present pursuant to the terms of the trust agreement, then the settlor had not abandoned sufficient control and dominion over the property to make the gift complete. Reversed.

▶ *ANALYSIS*

The donor has the primary liability for paying the gift tax, and if the donor does not pay, then the donee is liable for the unpaid gift tax. The executor or administrator of a decedent's estate has personal liability for payment of the estate tax but is only limited for reimbursement out of the decedent's estate. Persons in possession of the decedents property are liable for the tax due if there is no administration of the estate.

■=■

Quicknotes

GIFT TAX A tax levied on the transfer of property that is made as a gift.

SETTLOR The grantor or donor of property that is to be held in trust for the benefit of another.

■=■

Estate of Cristofani v. Commissioner

Trustee (P) v. Tax commissioner (D)

U.S.T.C., 97 T.C. 74 (1991).

NATURE OF CASE: Appeal from a disallowance of an annual gift exclusion.

FACT SUMMARY: After establishing an irrevocable trust for her two children and five grandchildren, Maria Cristofani claimed two $70,000 annual transfers to the trust qualified as annual exclusions under federal tax law.

🏛 RULE OF LAW

When a trust instrument gives a beneficiary the legal power to demand immediate possession of corpus, that power constitutes a present interest in property sufficient to qualify for a gift tax exclusion.

FACTS: Decedent Maria Cristofani established an irrevocable trust for her two children and five grandchildren. The parents were named as trustees (P) for the children's trust. All seven beneficiaries of the trust had the right to withdraw an annual amount not to exceed the amount specified for the federal gift tax exclusion, that is, up to $10,000. There was no agreement or understanding between Maria, the trustees (P), and the beneficiaries that the grandchildren would not immediately exercise their withdrawal rights. Thus, Maria did not report two $70,000 transfers to the trust, claiming them as seven annual exclusions for each of the applicable periods. The Commissioner (D) allowed the annual exclusions with respect to Maria's two children but disallowed the exclusions for the five grandchildren after determining that they were not transfers of present interests in property. Maria's estate (P) appealed.

ISSUE: When a trust instrument gives a beneficiary the legal power to demand immediate possession of corpus, does that power constitute a present interest in property?

HOLDING AND DECISION: (Ruwe, J.) Yes. When a trust instrument gives a beneficiary the legal power to demand immediate possession of corpus, that power constitutes a present interest in property sufficient to qualify for a gift tax exclusion. The likelihood that a beneficiary will actually receive present enjoyment of the property is not the test for determining whether a present interest has been received. In this case, each grandchild possessed the legal right to withdraw trust corpus, and the trustees would be unable to legally resist a grandchild's withdrawal demand. Moreover, based upon the provisions of the children's trust, Cristofani intended to benefit her grandchildren, contrary to the contention of the

Commissioner (D). Although the grandchildren never exercised their respective withdrawal rights, this does not vitiate the fact that they had the legal right to do so. Accordingly, the exclusions are allowed. Reversed.

▶ ANALYSIS

The court here relied on *Crummey v. Commissioner*, 397 F.2d 82 (9th Cir. 1968), which originally granted the gift tax shelter to beneficiaries with withdrawal powers. This case is important because it extends the annual exclusion to so-called *Crummey* power holders who are only contingent beneficiaries, like Maria's grandchildren. It is a victory for taxpayers because it supports an increased number of $10,000 tax-free gifts available to trustors.

■■▬■

Quicknotes

CORPUS The principal property comprising a trust, not including interest or income.

DONEE A person to whom a gift is made.

DURABLE POWER OF ATTORNEY A written document pursuant to which one party confers the authority to act as an agent on his behalf to another party and which is to become effective if the grantor should later become incapacitated.

FUTURE INTEREST An interest in property the right to possession or enjoyment of which is to take place at some time in the future.

GIFT TAX A tax levied on the transfer of property that is made as a gift.

REMAINDER INTEREST An interest in land that remains after the termination of the immediately preceding estate.

■■▬■

Estate of Maxwell v. Commissioner

Estate (P) v. Tax commissioner (D)

3 F.3d 591 (2nd Cir. 1993).

NATURE OF CASE: Appeal from assessment of estate tax deficiency.

FACT SUMMARY: When decedent transferred property to her son and his wife at the end of her life with the intention of remaining in possession so that he would not have to pay off a mortgage note executed in her favor, the Commissioner of the IRS (D) assessed a deficiency against her estate (P) when it reported only the unpaid balance on the note rather than the fair market value of the residence, which was twice as much.

> ## ⊞ RULE OF LAW
> The value of property disposed of during a decedent's lifetime shall be included in the gross estate where she has retained possession or enjoyment of it until her death and the transfer was not a bona fide sale for adequate and full consideration.

FACTS: Decedent, an eighty-two-year-old suffering from cancer, conveyed her personal residence of twenty-seven years to her son and only heir and his wife, the Maxwells, for $270,000. Decedent forgave $20,000 of the purchase price at the time of the transfer, and a note for $250,000 was executed in her favor. Simultaneously, the home was leased back to her for five years. Two days later, decedent executed a will with a provision forgiving the balance owing on the note at her death. After the transfer, she continued to live alone in the house until her death two years later. During that time, the rent payments by decedent functionally canceled out interest payments on the note paid by the Maxwells, and she forgave $20,000 on the note each year. Less than two months after her death, the house was sold for $550,000. On the decedent's estate tax return, the estate (P) reported only the $210,000 remaining on the debt. The IRS Commissioner (D) found that the transaction was a transfer with retained life estate and assessed an estate tax deficiency to adjust for the difference between the reported $210,000 and the fair market value of $550,000. The estate (P) appealed to the Tax Court. At oral argument, the estate (P) admitted that there was an intention among the parties that the mortgage note not be paid. The Tax Court affirmed the Commissioner's (D) ruling, and the estate (P) appealed.

ISSUE: Shall the value of property disposed of during a decedent's lifetime be included in the gross estate where she has retained possession or enjoyment of the property until her death and the transfer was not a bona fide sale for adequate and full consideration?

HOLDING AND DECISION: (Lasker, J.) Yes. The value of property disposed of during a decedent's lifetime shall be included in the gross estate where she has retained possession or enjoyment of it until her death, unless the transfer was a bona fide sale for adequate and full consideration. Possession or enjoyment of property is retained by the transferor when there is an express or implied understanding to that effect among the parties at the time of the transfer. The burden is on the decedent's estate to disprove the existence of any adverse implied agreement or understanding. The estate (P) has not met its burden in this case. Similarly, intent is a relevant inquiry in determining whether a transaction is bona fide. Where, as here, there is an implied agreement between the parties that the grantee would never be called upon to make any payments to the grantor, the note given by the grantee has no value at all. Therefore, the conveyance to the Maxwells was not a bona fide sale for an adequate and full consideration. Affirmed.

▌ *ANALYSIS*

The case above involved the application of § 2036(a) of the Internal Revenue Code. Section 2036(a) provides: "The value of the gross estate shall include the value of all property to the extent of any interest therein of which the decedent has at any time made a transfer (except in case of a bona fide sale for an adequate and full consideration in money or money's worth), by trust or otherwise, under which he has retained for his life or for any period which does not in fact end before his death—(1) The possession or enjoyment of, or the right to the income from, the property, or (2) The right, either alone or in conjunction with any person, to designate the persons who shall possess or enjoy the property or the income therefrom."

▬═▬

Quicknotes

BONA FIDE In good faith.

DECEDENT A person who is deceased.

CONSIDERATION Value given by one party in exchange for performance, or a promise to perform, by another party.

LIFE ESTATE An interest in land measured by the life of the tenant or a third party.

▬═▬

Old Colony Trust Co. v. United States

Estate Administrator (D) v. Government (P)

423 F.2d 601 (1st Cir. 1970).

NATURE OF CASE: Appeal from finding of estate tax deficiency.

FACT SUMMARY: Old Colony (D), the administrator of the estate of the unnamed decedent, contended that the estate should not be taxed on a trust established by the settlor which gave the trustee power to stop payments to the settlor's son at any time.

🏛 RULE OF LAW
The corpus of a trust included in an estate will not be fixed solely because the settlor named himself as trustee.

FACTS: The decedent, unnamed in the case, established an inter vivos trust prior to his death in which the initial life beneficiary of the trust was the settlor's adult son. Eighty percent of the income was normally to be payable to him and the balance added to the principal. Article 4 of the trust agreement permitted the trustees to increase the percentage of income payable to the son beyond the 80% "in their absolute discretion . . . when in their opinion such increase is needed in case of sickness, or desirable in view of changed circumstances." In addition, under Article 4 the trustees were given the discretion to cease paying income to the son and add it all to principal "during such period as the Trustees may decide that the stoppage of such payments is for his best interests." Article 7 gave the trustees broad administrative and management powers over the trust corpus. After the death of the settlor, who also had acted as the sole trustee of the trust, the government (P) sought to include the corpus of the trust in the estate of the settlor, contending that the settlor had possessed the ownership of the corpus because he could designate the persons who could enjoy its income and that until the date of his death he had an absolute right to alter, amend, or terminate the trust. After the trial court ruled for the government (P), the executor of the estate (D) appealed.

ISSUE: Will the corpus of a trust included in an estate not be taxed solely because the settlor named himself as trustee?

HOLDING AND DECISION: (Aldrich, J.) Yes. A settlor will not find the corpus of the trust included in his estate merely because he named himself a trustee. He must have reserved a power to himself that is inconsistent with the full termination of ownership. Trustee powers given for the administration or management of the trust must be equitably exercised for the benefit of the trust as a whole. It is difficult to see how a power can be subject to control by the probate court and exercisable only in what the trustee fairly concludes is in the interests of the trust and its beneficiaries as a whole and at the same time be an ownership power. However, under Article 4 of the trust, the trustees could increase the life tenant's income "in case of sickness, or . . . in view of changed circumstances." Alternatively, they could reduce it "for his best interests." Additional payments to a beneficiary whenever in his best interests is a broad standard, showing the plain indicia of ownership. With the present settlor-trustee free to determine the standard himself, a finding of ownership was warranted. To put it another way, the cost of holding onto the strings may prove to be a rope burn. Affirmed.

▶ ANALYSIS

In this case, the court held that the mere grant of administrative control to the trustees did not equate to indicia of ownership. In its decision, the court held that no aggregation of purely administrative powers can meet the government's amorphous test of "sufficient dominion and control" so as to be equated with ownership. The court also noted that trustee powers were not to be construed more broadly for tax purposes than a probate court would construe them for administrative purposes.

■■■

Quicknotes

INTER VIVOS TRUST Property that is held by one person for the benefit of another and which is created by an instrument that takes effect during the life of the grantor.

TRUST CORPUS The aggregate body of assets placed into a trust.

■■■

Estate of Vissering v. Commissioner

Trustees (P) v. Tax commissioner (D)

990 F.2d 578 (10th Cir. 1993).

NATURE OF CASE: Appeal from a judgment including the assets of a trust in the gross estate of a co-trustee.

FACT SUMMARY: Because the tax court determined that Vissering, at the time of his death, held a general power of appointment over the assets of a trust of which he was a cotrustee, the court included the assets of the trust in Vissering's gross estate (P) for federal estate tax purposes.

RULE OF LAW
A power vested in a trustee to invade the principal of the trust for his own benefit is sufficient to find the decedent trustee to have a general power of appointment, unless the power is limited by an ascertainable standard related to health, education, support, or maintenance.

FACTS: Vissering and a bank were cotrustees (P) of a trust created by his mother. The trust agreement authorized the trustees (P) to pay over, use, or expend, for the direct or indirect benefit of any of the beneficiaries, whatever amount or amounts of the principal of the trust as may, in the discretion of the trustees (P), be required for the continued comfort, support, maintenance, or education of said beneficiary. The tax court found that Vissering held a general power of appointment at the time of his death, and therefore, the assets of the trust were to be included in his gross estate for federal estate tax purposes. The estate (P) appealed.

ISSUE: Is a power vested in a trustee to invade the principal of the trust for his own benefit sufficient to find the decedent trustee to have a general power of appointment, unless the power is limited by an ascertainable standard related to health, education, support, or maintenance?

HOLDING AND DECISION: (Logan, C.J.) Yes. A power vested in a trustee to invade the principal of the trust for his own benefit is sufficient to find the decedent trustee to have a general power of appointment, unless the power is limited by an ascertainable standard related to health, education, support, or maintenance. A trust document permitting invasion of principal for comfort, without further qualifying language, creates a general power of appointment. However, there is modifying language in the trust at issue. "Comfort," in context, does not permit an unlimited power of invasion. Moreover, invasion of the corpus is permitted only to the extent "required," not to the extent "determined" or "desired."

Thus, the tax court erred in finding that Vissering had a general power of appointment includable in his estate (P). Reversed and remanded.

ANALYSIS

The court of appeals undertook a de novo review. Since the trust was created in Florida, specifying that Florida law controlled, the court of appeals looked to what it believed the Florida courts would hold. The estate (P) argued unsuccessfully that Vissering (P) was not a trustee at the time of death since he had been judged incapacitated by a New Mexico court.

Quicknotes

CONTINGENT BENEFICIARY A third party who is the recipient of the benefit of a transaction undertaken by another, the receipt of which is based on the uncertain happening of another event.

POWER OF APPOINTMENT Power, created by another person in connection with a gratuitous transfer (often in trust), residing in a person (as trustee or otherwise) to affect the disposition or distribution of the property.

REMAINDER BENEFICIARY A person who is to receive property that is held in trust after the termination of a preceding income interest.

Estate of Kurz v. Commissioner

Heirs (D) v. Internal Revenue Service (P)

68 F.3d 1027 (7th Cir. 1995).

NATURE OF CASE: Appeal from tax court ruling.

FACT SUMMARY: The IRS (P) claimed that certain trust assets should have been included for estate tax purposes because the beneficiary had full discretion to access the assets.

🏛 **RULE OF LAW**
Beneficiaries of multiple trusts cannot exclude trust assets from estate taxes by arranging the trusts in sequence.

FACTS: Ethel Kurz was the beneficiary of two trusts from 1971 to 1986. She was entitled to as much of the principal of the first trust (the marital trust) as she wanted, but could only take 5 percent of the family trust in any year, and only after the marital trust was exhausted. When she died, the tax court ruled that her power of appointment over 5 percent of the family trust required inclusion of that amount for purposes of estate taxes. The estate (D) claimed that this was wrong because the condition must actually be satisfied before Ethel had exercisable control over the portion of the family trust. Since the marital trust was not exhausted, the estate (D) claimed that no part of the family trust should have been included in the estate and appealed the tax court decision.

ISSUE: Can beneficiaries of multiple trusts exclude trust assets from estate taxes by arranging the trusts in sequence?

HOLDING AND DECISION: (Easterbrook, J.) No. Beneficiaries of multiple trusts cannot exclude trust assets from estate taxes by arranging the trusts in sequence. The law is designed to include in the taxable estate all assets that the decedent possessed or effectively controlled. If a beneficiary need only make a simple act or request to receive money or property, then power over the property is exercisable and should be included in the estate. The estate's (D) position on this matter would allow the creation of artificial mechanisms to avoid the tax implications. A trust could be divided into many funds, each of which couldn't be touched until the previous one was exhausted. Although the beneficiary could receive everything at once simply by requesting it, the estate (D) claims that the beneficiary really only has effective control over those funds that have actually been depleted. The key question is what funds the beneficiary has economic control over at any given moment. Without any other required or contingent events, Ethel Kurz had control over the entire marital trust and 5 percent of the family trust at any given moment before her death. Accordingly, those funds must be included within the estate (D) for tax purposes. Affirmed.

▶ **ANALYSIS**

The court spent much time in the decision distinguishing between contingent events and the type of actions involved in sequential trusts. Section 2041 of the Tax Code was the section at dispute in this case. The parties disagreed over the meaning of a regulation written to explain the law, but the court mostly went back to the common sense notion that the trust beneficiary obviously has control over any funds that can be accessed immediately.

■■■

Quicknotes

BENEFICIARY A third party who is the recipient of the benefit of a transaction undertaken by another.

■■■

Estate of Rapp v. Commissioner

Estate (P) v. Internal Revenue Service (D)

140 F.3d 1211 (1998).

NATURE OF CASE: Appeal from tax court ruling.

FACT SUMMARY: A California probate court reformed Rapp's will so that part of the estate (P) was tax exempt but the IRS (D) applied its own analysis.

🏛 RULE OF LAW
Federal tax courts are not bound by state probate rulings with regard to estate tax determinations.

FACTS: Bert Rapp died in 1988, survived by a wife and two children. His will left half his property to a trust, but the will did not create a qualified terminable interest property (QTIP) trust, which would have allowed Mrs. Rapp to deduct the trust property from the estate (P) for purposes of taxes. However, a California probate court reformed the will to create a QTIP trust. When the estate (P) filed a federal tax statement and claimed a QTIP trust deduction, the IRS sent a notice of deficiency. In the subsequent federal tax court proceeding, the court reviewed California law and determined that the reformation of the will was improper because there was no evidence to suggest that Rapp had really intended to create a QTIP trust. The tax court ruled for the IRS (D) and the estate (P) appealed.

ISSUE: Are federal tax courts bound by state probate rulings with regard to estate tax determinations?

HOLDING AND DECISION: (Fletcher, J.) No. Federal tax courts are not bound by state probate rulings with regard to estate tax determinations. Generally, the value of property passed directly from a testator to a surviving spouse is deducted before computing federal estate taxes. However, if the interest passing consists only of a life estate or terminable interest, the value is not deducted. One exception to this is if the terminable interest qualifies as a QTIP, in which case the surviving spouse can elect the marital deduction. In California, probate courts have the authority to modify or reform trusts under the appropriate circumstances. However, federal tax courts are not bound by res judicata and collateral estoppel from making its own determination on the validity of related deductions unless the state's highest court has definitively ruled on the case. In the present case, Rapp's estate (P) initiated the request to reform the will and trust directly for the purposes of affecting federal estate tax liability. The tax court was not bound by the state probate decision and properly applied the law itself, finding that the probate court holding was contrary to the state law. Accordingly, while the estate (P) is still entitled to the reformation of the trust, it is not entitled to receive the federal tax benefits of a QTIP trust. Affirmed.

▶ ANALYSIS

The estate (P) claimed that not allowing the QTIP deduction would create a split among circuit courts with regard to the measuring date of a QTIP. But the court insisted that it was only dealing with the narrow issue of whether the tax court was bound by the state probate decision. Since it wasn't, and ruled that there never was a QTIP trust, the measuring date issue never arose here.

■■■

Pond v. Pond

Trustee (P) v. Beneficiaries (D)

Mass. Sup. Jud. Ct., 678 N.E.2d 1321 (1997).

NATURE OF CASE: Action seeking reformation of a trust in probate court.

FACT SUMMARY: Pond's wife (P) sought to reform a trust that inadvertently thwarted his intent and left the property subject to federal tax liability.

🏛 **RULE OF LAW**
Trusts may be reformed to qualify for federal tax deductions if there was a clear intent by the settlor to establish such a qualifying trust and an error in the drafting of the trust.

FACTS: Sidney Pond executed a will in 1991 and established a revocable trust, naming himself and his wife (P) trustees on the same day. Virtually of his assets were then transferred to the trust. The trust provided that all of the income and principal was to be paid to Sidney (P) and his wife during Sidney's life. However, the trust made no provision for his wife (P) to receive the income or principal if she survived him. Instead, it only held that it would terminate upon the death of both and be distributed to their children. Sidney's will left his estate to the trust and gave his wife (P) the authority to elect to qualify the revocable trust for federal estate tax marital deductions. Without this deduction, the estate would have to pay $70,000 in taxes. The sum total of these provisions left Sidney's wife (P) with no assets after Sidney's death, and the trust also did not qualify for the marital tax deduction. Thus, Pond's wife (P) requested that the court reform the trust instrument to give effect to Sidney's intent. The beneficiaries, the Ponds' children (D), were named defendants but assented to the proposed reformation.

ISSUE: May trusts be reformed to qualify for federal tax deductions if there was a clear intent by the settlor to establish such a qualifying trust and an error in the drafting of the trust?

HOLDING AND DECISION: (Lynch, J.) Yes. Trusts may be reformed to qualify for federal tax deductions if there was a clear intent by the settlor to establish such a qualifying trust and an error in the drafting of the trust. The modification of a trust agreement to conform with a settlor's intent with respect to the marital deduction is a matter of state law. When the trust does not embody the settlor's intent due to a scrivener's error, it may be reformed on clear and convincing proof of mistake. When determining whether a mistake has been made, courts should look at the trust as a whole and the surrounding circumstances. In the present case, it is entirely clear that Sidney intended to qualify the trust for the marital deduction. The clause in the trust which expressly gave his wife (P) the right to elect the deduction shows this intent. Thus, it must have been a mistake for the trust not to include a clause that provided Pond's wife (P) with income for life upon his death. This clause would have qualified the trust for the deduction. Given the lack of any provision for his wife (P) in the trust, the fact that she had complete discretion over the trust assets during his life and the provisions of the will naming her executrix of the will, also demonstrate that it was plainly a mistake. Accordingly, it is completely proper to reform the trust to embody this intent. Remanded to the probate court for judgment consistent with this decision.

▶ **ANALYSIS**

The reformation of trusts to take advantage of tax deductions is a new concept in state law. Massachusetts is at the forefront of achieving this goal. It has a procedure where parties can go straight to the highest court so that federal tax courts will be bound by their decisions.

■━■

Quicknotes

SETTLOR The grantor or donor of property that is to be held in trust for the benefit of another.

■━■

Common Latin Words and Phrases Encountered in the Law

A FORTIORI: Because one fact exists or has been proven, therefore a second fact that is related to the first fact must also exist.

A PRIORI: From the cause to the effect. A term of logic used to denote that when one generally accepted truth is shown to be a cause, another particular effect must necessarily follow.

AB INITIO: From the beginning; a condition which has existed throughout, as in a marriage which was void ab initio.

ACTUS REUS: The wrongful act; in criminal law, such action sufficient to trigger criminal liability.

AD VALOREM: According to value; an ad valorem tax is imposed upon an item located within the taxing jurisdiction calculated by the value of such item.

AMICUS CURIAE: Friend of the court. Its most common usage takes the form of an amicus curiae brief, filed by a person who is not a party to an action but is nonetheless allowed to offer an argument supporting his legal interests.

ARGUENDO: In arguing. A statement, possibly hypothetical, made for the purpose of argument, is one made arguendo.

BILL QUIA TIMET: A bill to quiet title (establish ownership) to real property.

BONA FIDE: True, honest, or genuine. May refer to a person's legal position based on good faith or lacking notice of fraud (such as a bona fide purchaser for value) or to the authenticity of a particular document (such as a bona fide last will and testament).

CAUSA MORTIS: With approaching death in mind. A gift causa mortis is a gift given by a party who feels certain that death is imminent.

CAVEAT EMPTOR: Let the buyer beware. This maxim is reflected in the rule of law that a buyer purchases at his own risk because it is his responsibility to examine, judge, test, and otherwise inspect what he is buying.

CERTIORARI: A writ of review. Petitions for review of a case by the United States Supreme Court are most often done by means of a writ of certiorari.

CONTRA: On the other hand. Opposite. Contrary to.

CORAM NOBIS: Before us; writs of error directed to the court that originally rendered the judgment.

CORAM VOBIS: Before you; writs of error directed by an appellate court to a lower court to correct a factual error.

CORPUS DELICTI: The body of the crime; the requisite elements of a crime amounting to objective proof that a crime has been committed.

CUM TESTAMENTO ANNEXO, ADMINISTRATOR (ADMINISTRATOR C.T.A.): With will annexed; an administrator c.t.a. settles an estate pursuant to a will in which he is not appointed.

DE BONIS NON, ADMINISTRATOR (ADMINISTRATOR D.B.N.): Of goods not administered; an administrator d.b.n. settles a partially settled estate.

DE FACTO: In fact; in reality; actually. Existing in fact but not officially approved or engendered.

DE JURE: By right; lawful. Describes a condition that is legitimate "as a matter of law," in contrast to the term "de facto," which connotes something existing in fact but not legally sanctioned or authorized. For example, de facto segregation refers to segregation brought about by housing patterns, etc., whereas de jure segregation refers to segregation created by law.

DE MINIMUS: Of minimal importance; insignificant; a trifle; not worth bothering about.

DE NOVO: Anew; a second time; afresh. A trial de novo is a new trial held at the appellate level as if the case originated there and the trial at a lower level had not taken place.

DICTA: Generally used as an abbreviated form of obiter dicta, a term describing those portions of a judicial opinion incidental or not necessary to resolution of the specific question before the court. Such nonessential statements and remarks are not considered to be binding precedent.

DUCES TECUM: Refers to a particular type of writ or subpoena requesting a party or organization to produce certain documents in their possession.

EN BANC: Full bench. Where a court sits with all justices present rather than the usual quorum.

EX PARTE: For one side or one party only. An ex parte proceeding is one undertaken for the benefit of only one party, without notice to, or an appearance by, an adverse party.

EX POST FACTO: After the fact. An ex post facto law is a law that retroactively changes the consequences of a prior act.

EX REL.: Abbreviated form of the term ex relatione, meaning, upon relation or information. When the state brings an action in which it has no interest against an individual at the instigation of one who has a private interest in the matter.

FORUM NON CONVENIENS: Inconvenient forum. Although a court may have jurisdiction over the case, the action should be tried in a more conveniently located court, one to which parties and witnesses may more easily travel, for example.

GUARDIAN AD LITEM: A guardian of an infant as to litigation, appointed to represent the infant and pursue his/her rights.

HABEAS CORPUS: You have the body. The modern writ of habeas corpus is a writ directing that a person (body) being detained (such as a prisoner) be brought before the court so that the legality of his detention can be judicially ascertained.

IN CAMERA: In private, in chambers. When a hearing is held before a judge in his chambers or when all spectators are excluded from the courtroom.

IN FORMA PAUPERIS: In the manner of a pauper. A party who proceeds in forma pauperis because of his poverty is one who is allowed to bring suit without liability for costs.

INFRA: Below, under. A word referring the reader to a later part of a book. (The opposite of supra.)

IN LOCO PARENTIS: In the place of a parent.

IN PARI DELICTO: Equally wrong; a court of equity will not grant requested relief to an applicant who is in pari delicto, or as much at fault in the transactions giving rise to the controversy as is the opponent of the applicant.

IN PARI MATERIA: On like subject matter or upon the same matter. Statutes relating to the same person or things are said to be in pari materia. It is a general rule of statutory construction that such statutes should be construed together, i.e., looked at as if they together constituted one law.

IN PERSONAM: Against the person. Jurisdiction over the person of an individual.

IN RE: In the matter of. Used to designate a proceeding involving an estate or other property.

IN REM: A term that signifies an action against the res, or thing. An action in rem is basically one that is taken directly against property, as distinguished from an action in personam, i.e., against the person.

INTER ALIA: Among other things. Used to show that the whole of a statement, pleading, list, statute, etc., has not been set forth in its entirety.

INTER PARTES: Between the parties. May refer to contracts, conveyances or other transactions having legal significance.

INTER VIVOS: Between the living. An inter vivos gift is a gift made by a living grantor, as distinguished from bequests contained in a will, which pass upon the death of the testator.

IPSO FACTO: By the mere fact itself.

JUS: Law or the entire body of law.

LEX LOCI: The law of the place; the notion that the rights of parties to a legal proceeding are governed by the law of the place where those rights arose.

MALUM IN SE: Evil or wrong in and of itself; inherently wrong. This term describes an act that is wrong by its very nature, as opposed to one which would not be wrong but for the fact that there is a specific legal prohibition against it (malum prohibitum).

MALUM PROHIBITUM: Wrong because prohibited, but not inherently evil. Used to describe something that is wrong because it is expressly forbidden by law but that is not in and of itself evil, e.g., speeding.

MANDAMUS: We command. A writ directing an official to take a certain action.

MENS REA: A guilty mind; a criminal intent. A term used to signify the mental state that accompanies a crime or other prohibited act. Some crimes require only a general mens rea (general intent to do the prohibited act), but others, like assault with intent to murder, require the existence of a specific mens rea.

MODUS OPERANDI: Method of operating; generally refers to the manner or style of a criminal in committing crimes, admissible in appropriate cases as evidence of the identity of a defendant.

NEXUS: A connection to.

NISI PRIUS: A court of first impression. A nisi prius court is one where issues of fact are tried before a judge or jury.

N.O.V. (NON OBSTANTE VEREDICTO): Not withstanding the verdict. A judgment n.o.v. is a judgment given in favor of one party despite the fact that a verdict was returned in favor of the other party, the justification being that the verdict either had no reasonable support in fact or was contrary to law.

NUNC PRO TUNC: Now for then. This phrase refers to actions that may be taken and will then have full retroactive effect.

PENDENTE LITE: Pending the suit; pending litigation underway.

PER CAPITA: By head; beneficiaries of an estate, if they take in equal shares, take per capita.

PER CURIAM: By the court; signifies an opinion ostensibly written "by the whole court" and with no identified author.

PER SE: By itself, in itself; inherently.

PER STIRPES: By representation. Used primarily in the law of wills to describe the method of distribution where a person, generally because of death, is unable to take that which is left to him by the will of another, and therefore his heirs divide such property between them rather than take under the will individually.

PRIMA FACIE: On its face, at first sight. A prima facie case is one that is sufficient on its face, meaning that the evidence supporting it is adequate to establish the case until contradicted or overcome by other evidence.

PRO TANTO: For so much; as far as it goes. Often used in eminent domain cases when a property owner receives partial payment for his land without prejudice to his right to bring suit for the full amount he claims his land to be worth.

QUANTUM MERUIT: As much as he deserves. Refers to recovery based on the doctrine of unjust enrichment in those cases in which a party has rendered valuable services or furnished materials that were accepted and enjoyed by another under circumstances that would reasonably notify the recipient that the rendering party expected to be paid. In essence, the law implies a contract to pay the reasonable value of the services or materials furnished.

QUASI: Almost like; as if; nearly. This term is essentially used to signify that one subject or thing is almost analogous to another but that material differences between them do exist. For example, a quasi-criminal proceeding is one that is not strictly criminal but shares enough of the same characteristics to require some of the same safeguards (e.g., procedural due process must be followed in a parole hearing).

QUID PRO QUO: Something for something. In contract law, the consideration, something of value, passed between the parties to render the contract binding.

RES GESTAE: Things done. In evidence law, this principle justifies the admission of a statement that would otherwise be hearsay when it is made so closely to the event in question as to be said to be a part of it, or with such spontaneity as not to have the possibility of falsehood.

RES IPSA LOQUITUR: The thing speaks for itself. This doctrine gives rise to a rebuttable presumption of negligence when the instrumentality causing the injury was within the exclusive control of the defendant, and the injury was one that does not normally occur unless a person has been negligent.

RES JUDICATA: A matter adjudged. Doctrine which provides that once a court of competent jurisdiction has rendered a final judgment or decree on the merits, that judgment or decree is conclusive upon the parties to the case and prevents them from engaging in any other litigation on the points and issues determined therein.

RESPONDEAT SUPERIOR: Let the master reply. This doctrine holds the master liable for the wrongful acts of his servant (or the principal for his agent) in those cases in which the servant (or agent) was acting within the scope of his authority at the time of the injury.

STARE DECISIS: To stand by or adhere to that which has been decided. The common law doctrine of stare decisis attempts to give security and certainty to the law by following the policy that once a principle of law as applicable to a certain set of facts has been set forth in a decision, it forms a precedent that will subsequently be followed, even though a different decision might be made were it the first time the question had arisen. Of course, stare decisis is not an inviolable principle and is departed from in instances where there is good cause (e.g., considerations of public policy led the Supreme Court to disregard prior decisions sanctioning segregation).

SUPRA: Above. A word referring a reader to an earlier part of a book.

ULTRA VIRES: Beyond the power. This phrase is most commonly used to refer to actions taken by a corporation that are beyond the power or legal authority of the corporation.

Addendum of French Derivatives

IN PAIS: Not pursuant to legal proceedings.

CHATTEL: Tangible personal property.

CY PRES: Doctrine permitting courts to apply trust funds to purposes not expressed in the trust but necessary to carry out the settlor's intent.

PER AUTRE VIE: For another's life; during another's life. In property law, an estate may be granted that will terminate upon the death of someone other than the grantee.

PROFIT A PRENDRE: A license to remove minerals or other produce from land.

VOIR DIRE: Process of questioning jurors as to their predispositions about the case or parties to a proceeding in order to identify those jurors displaying bias or prejudice.

Casenote Legal Briefs